Mountain Biking
NEW HAMPSHIRE

Mountain Biking
NEW HAMPSHIRE

A Guide to the Best 25 Places to Ride

by Stuart Johnstone
photographs by the author

Active Publications
P.O. Box 716
Carlisle, MA 01741-0716

Trails and conditions may change over time, so we would appreciate hearing corrections you find. Your opinions and suggestions are also welcome.
Please address them to:

Active Publications
P.O. Box 716
Carlisle, MA 01741-0716

Published by :
    Active Publications
    P.O. Box 716
    Carlisle, MA 01741-0716

Printed in the United States of America

Publisher's Cataloging in Publication Data

Johnstone, Stuart A.
    Mountain Biking New Hampshire: A Guide to the Best 25 Places to Ride / by Stuart A. Johnstone; photographs by the author.
    2nd edition, revised
     ISBN 0-9627990-0-9
    1. All-terrain cycling - New Hampshire - Guide-books. 2. New Hampshire - Description and travel
    Library of Congress Catalog Card Number: 92-74375

Acknowledgements

This has been a long and challenging journey, and it would not have been possible without the encouragement which I received along the way. I am grateful to all who helped, in some way, to keep my wheels rolling.

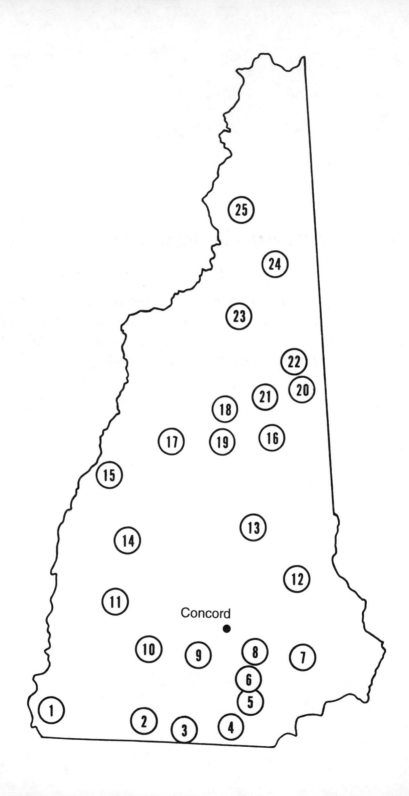

Contents

Introduction

Mountain Biking New Hampshire

The Granite State is famous for outdoor adventure. Its brilliant mountains, grand lakes, and vast forests draw visitors seeking a refreshment which only nature can provide. And its abundant trails and backcountry roads provide a paradise for off-road bicyclists, who can enjoy this beautiful scenery while they ride. Between nearby parks in the Merrimack Valley and spectacular routes in the White Mountains, the possibilities rank among New England's best.

Mountain biking is an ideal synthesis of physical exercise and outdoor enjoyment. Across the country, people are discovering the undeniable satisfaction of pedaling a bicycle in concert with the peace and quiet of the natural world. Enthusiasm comes from road riders frustrated by the noise, fumes, and safety hazards of car traffic, from hikers intrigued by the smoothness of pedaling and the freedom to access remote places, and even from skiers, both downhill and cross country, who find it a worthy substitute while waiting for snow. It has become a favorite way to enjoy the countryside and back woods of New Hampshire.

The best 25 places to ride come in many forms and include national forest lands, state parks and forests, and locally owned areas. Several locations center on public roads which remain unpaved and, in places, unmaintained. This guide describes them for all ability levels and offers the directions and suggestions for a great ride. Providing current trail policy information and accurate maps, it is a complete resource for New Hampshire's mountain biking opportunities.

Trail Manners

Trail access, especially in high-use areas, is now threatened by careless riding habits. Complaints from both land managers and other trail users have sent a clear signal on a variety of preventable problems. Tomorrow's policies are shaped by the actions of today's riders, so it is extremely important that mountain bicyclists respect the concerns of other trail users, the problems of soil erosion, and the importance of coexisting in the trail community. In hopes of securing trail access by educating riders, the International Mountain Bicycling Association has adopted the following guidelines:

IMBA Rules of the Trail

1. Ride on open trails only. Respect trail and road closures (ask if not sure), avoid possible trespass on private land, obtain permits and authorization as may be required. Federal and state wilderness areas are closed to cycling.

2. Leave no trace. Be sensitive to the dirt beneath you. Even on open trails, you should not ride under conditions where you will leave evidence of your passing, such as on certain soils shortly after a rain. Observe the different types of soils and trail construction; practice low-impact cycling. This also means staying on the trail and not creating any new ones. Be sure to pack out at least as much as you pack in.

3. Control your bicycle! Inattention for even a second can cause disaster. Excessive speed maims and threatens people; there is no excuse for it!

4. Always yield the trail. Make known your approach well in advance. A friendly greeting (or bell) is considerate and works well; startling someone may cause loss of trail access. Show your respect when passing others by slowing to a walk or even stopping. Anticipate that other trail users may be around corners or in blind spots.

5. Never spook animals. All animals are startled by an unannounced approach, a sudden movement or a loud noise. This can be dangerous for you, for others and for the animals. Give animals extra room and time to adjust to you. In passing, use special care and follow the directions of horseback riders (ask if uncertain). Running cattle and disturbing wild animals is a serious offense. Leave gates as you found them, or as marked.

6. Plan ahead. Know your equipment, your ability and the area in which you are riding -- and prepare accordingly. Be self-sufficient at all times. Wear a helmet, keep your machine in good condition, and carry necessary supplies for changes in weather or other conditions. A well executed trip is a satisfaction to you and not a burden or offense to others.

Certain aspects of these rules deserve emphasis, especially in regards to the heavily used trails of the Northeast. Most importantly, never ride when conditions are wet because ruts will form easily and soils will erode. Allow a few days to pass before riding after a heavy rain. Be aware that mountain biking on trails is discouraged or, at some locations, strictly forbidden in spring when the ground is thawing and vulnerable to even the most conscientious low-impact cycling. Keep to the pavement or well-drained gravel roads until mud season has past, typically by mid-May but later in the White Mountains. Land managers point out that all forms of trail use lead to erosion, and that visitors should focus on minimizing this damage.

When crossing streams, especially those with silty or muddy bottoms, dismount your bike and walk across to prevent unnecessary disruption. And when crossing puddles or mudholes it is best to either ride or walk through the center rather than to circle the edge and further widen the trail. Since every situation is different, use your judgement about what is the least disruptive course to take.

Never skid! Not only does it disrupt the soil but it also

leaves a very visible, negative image for other trail users.

Horses are easily frightened by mountain bikes. With relatively poor eyesight and only *flight or fight* instincts, they are prone to panic when a bicycle approaches quickly, quietly, and without warning, creating a potentially dangerous situation. When passing a horse communicate with the rider well in advance, especially if coming from the rear. Be willing to stop your bike and accept the equestrian's instructions for proceeding.

Many trails in New Hampshire, especially the vast network of snowmobile routes crisscrossing the state, pass over private lands and may or may not be open to the public in summer. Respect private property by getting the permission of landowners first.

Pedaling softly means riding on trails in a way that allows you to return to them another day. Be sensitive to the soil surface beneath you, remember the concerns of a hiker at a blind corner, and understand that trails are a limited and very valuable resource. Educate others about good riding habits and the importance of preventing trail closures, and whenever possible give back to your favorite trails by volunteering for maintenance. Help secure the future by demonstrating that mountain bikes can be ridden safely with minimal impact on the environment.

Trail Policies

Banned from many of the country's public lands, mountain biking is not an acceptable activity on every trail. While bicyclists are welcomed in most of New Hampshire's parklands, restrictions do exist at various locations and it is important to understand and respect them. Be alert for trailhead notices regarding current trail policies since conditions can change.

White Mountain National Forest roads and trails offer many riding opportunities, but not all are open or suited for bicycling. The Appalachian Trail and designated

Wilderness Areas are strictly off-limits. Although all other trails are technically open to bicycling, the National Forest staff advises that careful judgement be used in regards to hiking traffic, terrain, and overall trail conditions. Note that the boundaries of the National Forest are clearly delineated by red tree blazes. For further information contact the White Mountain National Forest, Box 638, Laconia, NH 03246, Tel. (603) 528-8721. Regional offices and information centers are located throughout the area.

New Hampshire state parks and forests comprise a vast array of lands ranging from isolated woodlands like Nash Stream State Forest to heavily visited places like Bear Brook State Park. The official policy permits bicycle usage on all trails unless they are posted otherwise, but bicycles and wheeled vehicles are restricted from state park roads and trails until May 23 each year. Since each area has its own policies regarding bicycling, always read trailhead notices for current information. Volunteers interested in trail maintenance projects should contact park or forest supervisors for opportunities. Property boundaries at state parks and forests are marked by blue tree blazes. For further information contact the New Hampshire Department of Resources and Economic Development, Division of Parks and Recreation, P.O. Box 856, Concord, NH 03301-0856, Tel. (603) 271-3254 or the Division of Forests and Lands at (603) 271-3457.

Locally-owned lands are subject to rules of the conservation commissions or parks departments of the community. Since each has its own expectations and concerns, be sensitive to the general usage and ride accordingly.

All areas ask that visitors not block trailhead gates when parking because work crews and emergency vehicles always need access.

Planning Your Ride

Getting lost or injured, underestimating trip length or difficulty, and overestimating your own strength or skill level can bring dire consequences in the far reaches of the woods. A weather change or bicycle failure can ruin an otherwise wonderful ride. Be prepared for the worst by bringing some important items.

Drinking water is essential to remember. It is easy to become dehydrated while mountain biking because of the high level of exertion and constant cooling breeze, so start drinking before you get thirsty. Carry at least one water bottle on the frame or in a fanny pack and use it often. Many of the longer tours mentioned in this book could require several water bottles, especially in the heat of summer. Water taken from streams should be filtered, boiled, or chemically treated before drinking, even when far away from civilization. Although they may look appealing, mountain streams often harbor infectious bacteria such as *Giardia lamblia*, spread when human and animal wastes are deposited near streams. Be careful not to contribute to the problem.

Even if you are not planning a picnic, bring along something to eat in case your body runs low on fuel. A high-energy snack can provide an important boost both physically and psychologically on a long ride.

Always carry a map if you are unsure of the trails you plan to ride, and keep track of the route you follow. Remember that a 15-minute descent could require an hour-long return. Following the mileage directions of tours will require a cyclometer, a tiny trip computer which operates on a magnetic signal from the front wheel. It mounts on the handlebars to display distance, time, speed, and other useful information, and will bring valuable assistance when exploring a new area.

Be prepared with bug repellent during spring and summer when black flies and mosquitoes can be a

8

disastrous element to a day in the woods. Also consider extra clothing and rain gear, especially in the White Mountains where abrupt weather changes make hypothermia a year-round concern. A first-aid kit is also wise. These items add only minimal amounts of weight relative to their potential reward and can be carried either on the body or in a bike pack.

Mountain biking is discouraged at many areas during the late fall when New Hampshire's deer hunting season is underway. Most agree that it is wise to stay out of the woods altogether at this time.

Finally, ride with a companion, especially in remote areas of the White Mountains where help is far away. Leave word of your destination with a responsible person.

Bike Tools

Mountain bikes are built for abuse but still require regular maintenance and repairs, so it is smart to carry some basic tools and to know how to use them. Repairing a flat tire can be done with either a spare inner tube or a patch kit complete with sanding paper, patches, and glue, along with a pump which can attach securely to the bike's frame. Bring tire irons to help remove the tire from the rim, a set of allen wrenches and screw drivers to tighten or adjust the bolts holding various bike parts together, and a spoke tightener to adjust spokes or remove those that break. A chain tool is necessary to repair chains when links break or bend, and it can save the day so be sure to understand how it works. All of these tools and supplies can be carried in a small bike pack fitted either under the seat, on the frame, or in front of the handlebars.

Many of the trails listed in this book are remote so it is extremely important that your bike be well-tuned and properly maintained. If you are not capable of making general repairs on the trail and are not self-sufficient with tools, ride with others who are.

The Equipment

Mountain bikes are available in a large number of makes, models, and designs with a myriad of features. Your local bicycle stores can best explain the options. The important distinction is between *mountain bike* and *city bike*, for the two are closely related but not the same. Mountain bikes have stronger frames, wider tires, and higher quality components, making them better suited to off-road use. Most models come with twenty-one speeds, providing a gear for just about any situation.

The finely tuned and expensive components on a mountain bike will wear and corrode with use so protect your equipment with routine maintenance. Clean the bike after every ride if dirt and sand have accumulated on it because the debris will grind away at each moving part and shorten its life. Rinsing the chain, chainrings, and derailleurs with water and applying a bicycle lubricant will usually suffice, but sometimes a more serious scrubbing is required. Bearings, derailleur cables, and even the seatpost should be kept clean and well-greased so they will remain moveable. And remember to adjust the brake pads as they wear, so they do not rub unevenly or start to touch the tire instead of the rim.

What to Wear

The most important item is a helmet. Light in weight and comfortable to wear, it is now considered to be a bicyclist's best friend and valuable protection against the trees, rocks, and other objects along the trail. Since three quarters of all bicycle deaths result from head injuries, wearing a helmet is a healthy habit. Protective eye glasses or shields are also a good idea for overhanging tree branches.

Just about anything will do for clothes, but bring enough layers to suit possible weather changes. Bike shorts are a great advantage because the elastic material fits close to the body to eliminate chafing, and the padded crotch can save the day on long rides. In colder weather, full-length bicycle pants and a windbreaker are a good match.

Gell-filled gloves are effective at absorbing the bumps and vibrations of the trail and also help prevent numbness in the hands, a common condition for bicyclists. Mountain biking shoes are designed with firm soles and gripping treads to transmit maximum power to the pedal, but are still comfortable for hiking should you need to walk some areas.

About the Guidebook

Mountain biking is a sport meant for exploration. This guidebook serves as a stepping stone, preparing riders with trail descriptions, suggested destinations, and interesting background information. Maps are included to give a general description of trail networks and natural features, but plan to use U.S. Geological Survey maps (listed with each location) for mountainous and remote rides. Note that the map scale for each area varies widely, so plan your course carefully.

Specific terms are used to describe trails. Single-track refers to a trail width for just one rider, such as a footpath, while double-track refers to width for two or more bicyclists riding side by side, such as a woods road. Some double-track trails become overgrown with tall grass in summer and could appear as single-tracks. Gravel roads signify unpaved routes which are generally passable by car.

A three-grade rating system is used to define levels of trail difficulty. Hills, corners, trail surfaces, and obstacles like rocks and logs contribute to this rating. Easy applies to routes suitable for beginners, with gentle terrain and smooth, open surfaces. Intermediate refers to trails with moderate hills and avoidable rocks, roots, and other obstacles. Difficult describes those with steep hills and rugged, technical surfaces. Be careful to select routes which suit your level of skill and physical strength, or be willing to walk the difficult sections.

Practical information accompanies each description. In addition to relevant U.S. Geological Survey maps this includes sources of additional information and nearby bike shops for quick access to parts and service. Driving directions originate from major highways and will be most effective when used with a road map. Each site has only the major parking areas displayed on the trail map, so smaller areas could also exist.

Disclaimer

The author and Active Publications bear no liability for accidents, injuries, losses, or damages caused directly or indirectly by people engaged in the activities described in this book. It is the responsibility of every off-road bicyclist to ride with safety and consideration.

Mountain Biking

NEW HAMPSHIRE

A Guide to the Best 25 Places to Ride

1
Pisgah State Park
Winchester

Hidden in the hills of southwestern New Hampshire is one of the state's best-kept secrets. A sprawling woodland known as *Pisgy* to locals, the 13,000-acre park remains largely undeveloped and offers all the solitude of a northern wilderness. The mountain biking includes all levels of riding, from easy cruising on gravel roads to difficult maneuvering on eroded wagon tracks.

The park is fortunate to have a well-organized base of support from the local community, the Friends of Pisgah. The group helps with the purchase of additional lands, organizes trail maintenance, and coordinates a variety of hikes and outings throughout the year. Although the park has few amenities, trail intersection numbers have been placed at many locations to assist visitors in using the map and signs provide trail names and distances at major junctions. No fees are charged, but camping and fires are prohibited. Pisgah attracts a wide range of activities and the staff asks that all visitors respect other trail users and treat the area's natural resources with care.

Mountain biking is permitted only on gravel roads and woods roads at Pisgah, and is prohibited on all hiking trails. Signs at trailheads reading *Wheeled Vehicles Prohibited* refer to bicycles, in addition to off-road motorcycles and cars which have access to certain routes in the park. Although this limits the choices for cyclists, the large scale of the area and remoteness of many destinations leaves plenty of great riding. Also note that Pisgah is closed to bicycles and motor vehicles until May 23 each year so the ground can thaw and drain without excess disruption. Please respect these trail use regulations so that mountain bikes will continue to be welcome at the park.

Pisgah is accessible from all directions but the main route through the property is historic **Old Chesterfield Road**. Bordered by miles of stone walls which stretch through the woods, it was an important route for settlers who arrived in the late 1700's to build homes and clear the land. Today all that remains of their efforts is a collection of cellarholes and small cemeteries. Signs beside the road now mark the homesites of Jediah Eaton, Ebenezer Hutchins, and others. The foundation of a cider mill built around 1800 is another landmark, still surrounded by ancient apple trees.

Old Chesterfield Road remains a primary route for many forms of travel as it bisects the park over the course of 6 miles, linking the towns of **Winchester** and **Chesterfield**. Access is controlled by a gate near the park boundary on the Winchester side, which is locked each night during summer and closed throughout winter and spring. Roadside parking is available at many trail intersections along the way but be careful not to block other vehicles. From the gate bicyclists can ride for 2.3 miles on a gravel surface while enjoying the open scenery of beaver ponds and wetlands. Beyond Intersection 10 the road degrades to a trail for a rougher ride, rises steadily to Intersection 14, then rolls through the woods before ascending to the park's boundary at the end of **Winchester Road** in Chesterfield. **Horseshoe Road** bears right at a fork before this point, just below an abandoned farm field, and gradually climbs for a half-mile to another parking area where an expansive view spills over the park's hills and dales. This highpoint makes a rewarding destination on a clear day. A stone memorial nearby distinguishes it as the birthplace of former Supreme Court Chief Justice Harlan F. Stone.

Unfortunately 1300-foot **Mount Pisgah** is off-limits for bicyclists because it is reached only by footpaths, but its 300-foot cliff and distant views make it a popular hiking trip. Pisgah, a Biblical name, is the mountain in Jordan from

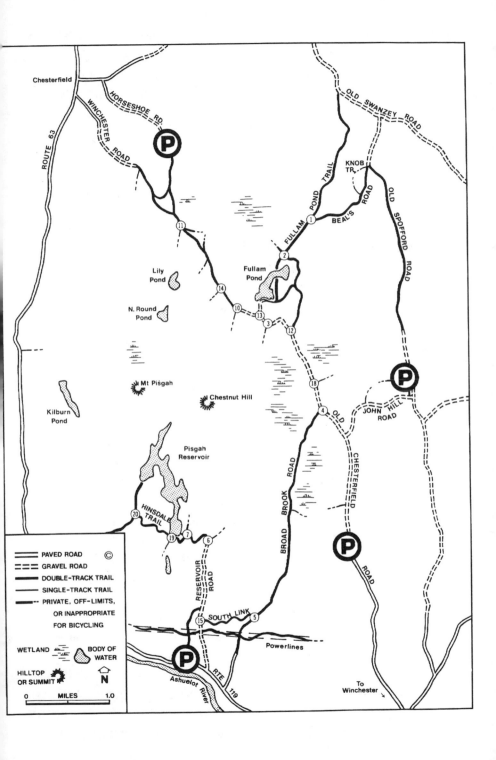

which Moses viewed the promised land, and settlers thought it a fitting name for the mountain overlooking their new homes. Many other single-tracks intersect Old Chesterfield Road and lead to places like **Lily Pond** and **North Round Pond** but all are off-limits to bicycling.

Stop for a rest at **Fullam Pond** where tall pines shade the shoreline. The water is accessible by road and is a popular place for canoeing in summer, but its muddy bottom spoils the swimming. The remains of a saw mill are located at the pond's southeastern corner. Though the dam has recently been rebuilt with concrete much of the original stonework can still be admired.

The **Fullam Pond Trail** was once the main street through Nash City, a tiny hill village also known as Hardscrabble after its poor, rocky soil. Although it starts as a fairly flat and smooth ride beside a peacefully flowing brook, the route degrades as it rises on a long uphill with a burdensome surface of loose rocks. It is 1.5 miles from Old Chesterfield Road to Intersection 1, where Fullam Pond Trail continues northward over a hill to **Old Swanzey Road** and **Beal's Road** forks right. A very difficult ascent, Beal's Road is spiced with the same loose rocks which gave Hardscrabble its name and requires bicyclists to pedal skillfully. A third of a mile from Fullam Pond Trail the old road passes the Latham-Beal Cemetery, which records the village's life from 1790 to its abandonment in 1885. The cemetery sits as a lonely relic, clinging to a rocky hillside deep in the forest. Beal's Road finally crests the hill at an intersection with **Knob Trail**, which climbs briefly to the top of Knob Hill for an easterly view to Mount Monadnock. This trail is off-limits to bicycles but worth the short hike.

Old Spofford Road intersects Beal's Road below this hill and offers an equally difficult option for continuing the ride. Lying outside the park's bounds, it is still a public road but no longer maintained. The stone walls and cellarholes along the way speak to a time when it had a more important purpose, but today a combination of eroded hills, deep ruts, and steadfast beaver dams give it a forgotten appearance. The presence of several private, side trails adds some confusion to riding this adventurous route. Ride Old Spofford Road only when you have plenty of time, lots of energy, and dry conditions.

The road gradually becomes more civilized a few miles to the south and is passable by car a half-mile before the parking lot near **John Hill Road**, a return route to Old Chesterfield Road. Once paved, John Hill Road is now crumbling away but the remaining surface makes the pedaling easier as the road rolls up and down short hills. It winds for a mile past cellarholes and overgrown meadows, once productive farm fields. Turning right on Old Chesterfield Road and returning to Fullam Pond completes a challenging, 8-mile loop with Fullam Pond Trail, Beal's Road, and Old Spofford Road.

Broad Brook Road is another old wagon road now used for a variety of outdoor activities. A rough surface slows the pedaling in places as the road stretches for over 3 miles between Old Chesterfield Road and **Route 119**. It descends on a southerly course following the flow of Broad Brook to the **Ashuelot River**, only 4 miles from its confluence with the Connecticut. Look for a rough trail beneath the **powerlines**, which traverse the many steep hills and valleys beside the Ashuelot River. Some pitches are barely rideable. Many of the hilltops on this tree-less corridor allow western views to the Green Mountains of Vermont, but private lands eventually block travel in both directions.

Gentler **South Link** is an easy way to connect Broad Brook Road with **Reservoir Road**, the park's southern gateway from Route 119. This gravel road begins at the river and climbs steeply out of the valley, then rolls peacefully through evergreen forest for 1.5 miles to a small parking area. From this point it climbs in switchbacks up another steep grade with the help of pavement, which provides bicyclists with much needed traction. The road narrows as it tucks in among shady hemlocks and cool rock ledges, then crests and descends to **Pisgah Reservoir**, an isolated pond banked by a pretty combination of ledge and pine. Two small dams contain the pond.

Cross the brook by the first dam, or use the bridge downstream if the water level is high, and continue past the second dam to reach the **Hinsdale Trail**, a narrower challenge of roots, rocks, and rough log bridges. It stretches for a couple of miles before leaving the park for private property, passing through a low marshland along the way. A spur at Intersection 20 reaches an isolated arm of the reservoir.

Driving Directions:

From Route 10 in Keene drive south to the center of Winchester. Turn right at the traffic light downtown, cross the bridge and continue up the hill to a five-way intersection. Continue straight across on Old Chesterfield Road and drive for 2.5 miles to where the pavement ends, near the park boundary. A gate farther up the road is open during daylight hours to provide access to Fullam Pond.

To reach the trailhead near Reservoir Road, continue south on Route 10 to Route 119. Turn right (west) and continue for 3 miles to the parking area at a state park sign on the right. This trailhead is 2 miles east of the village of Hinsdale.

Bike Shops:

Andy's Cycle Shop, 165 Winchester St., Keene, (603) 352-3410

Banagan's Cycling Company, 82 Main St., Keene, (603) 357-2331

Brattleboro Bicycle Shop, 178 Main St., Brattleboro, VT, (802) 254-8644

Summers Backcountry Sports, 16 Asheulot St., Keene, (603) 357-5107

USGS Maps:

Keene Quadrangle

Additional Information:

Pisgah State Park, P. O. Box 242, Winchester, NH 03470, Tel. (603) 239-8153

Friends of Pisgah, Inc., P. O. Box 144, West Swanzey, NH 03470

2
Annett State Forest
Rindge

Judging by its obscure trailhead, Annett State Forest appears to be little more than a picnic area but miles of nearby trails and gravel roads offer excellent opportunities for mountain biking. Only a stone's throw from Mount Monadnock, the riding spreads over rolling hills with both single-tracks and double-tracks exploring the forest's many hidden corners. A series of wetlands and ponds provide unique scenery and expansive wildlife habitat, making Annett a favorite spot for bird watchers, fishermen, and anyone else out to enjoy the peaceful outdoors of southern New Hampshire.

One of the state's oldest preserves, this forest originated in 1922 with Albert Annett's donation of 1300 acres of land. Though its well-worn roads and trails reach many areas, keep in mind that some extend beyond the state-owned boundaries and neighboring landowners might not appreciate visitors. Some specifically exclude bicycle usage from their trails. Keep a sharp eye for the state forest boundaries, blazed in blue, and respect private property.

The main route through Annett is **Hubbard Pond Road**, a public way which is no longer maintained by the town of Rindge. It is suitable for four wheel drive vehicles only and officially closed during the winter months. A few of the hills along the old road are rough from erosion but most of this 2-mile ride is easy pedaling, enhanced by a natural display of ponds, bogs, and deep forest. The road begins in Jaffrey where it is known as Annette Road, then shortly before passing **Black Reservoir** enters Rindge as Hubbard Pond Road and stretches eastward to New Ipswich, where it is passable by car.

Although Hubbard Pond Road existed long before the Great Depression, it is the backbone to a series of fire roads built by the Civilian Conservation Corps (CCC). Camp Annett, as it was called, housed 200 men and was located in the meadow at the **Annett Wayside**, a picnic area. In its four years of work in the area the CCC's progress included not only construction of the these fire roads but also significant reforestation, as the vast stands of red pine attest. The Corps also blazed many of the hiking trails on nearby Mount Monadnock, now distinguished as the second-most climbed mountain in the world.

These fire roads are generally easy riding in the shade of evergreen forests. Quieted by a smooth carpet of needles and lined by countless rows of red pine, they cruise through the undulating woods with peace and quiet but unfortunately either dead end or lead onto private property. Some make appealing side trips to surrounding wetlands or remote coves on **Hubbard Pond**, where the unspoiled shoreline reveals only a few houses. Others extend northward toward **Route 124** and the adjoining **Perry Reservation**, a property owned by the Society for the Preservation of New Hampshire Forests, where bicycling is not permitted.

An unnamed gravel road forks from Hubbard Pond Road and crosses the **dam** containing Hubbard Pond, then continues on a gentle rise back to **Cathedral Road**. Although crossing the stream below the dam requires a carry, the pedaling on this forest road is smooth and easy. Riders can combine it with Cathedral Road and Hubbard Pond Road for a 2-mile loop, ideal for beginners or those interested in familiarizing themselves with the area's network of options. The adjacent **Sawdust Trail** rolls through the woods in complete solitude and a more forgotten atmosphere, as tree branches reach out to claim its open space. Eventually it reaches the blue tree blazes of the state forest boundary, where it continues onto private land toward the Boy Scouts of America's **Camp Quinapoxet**,

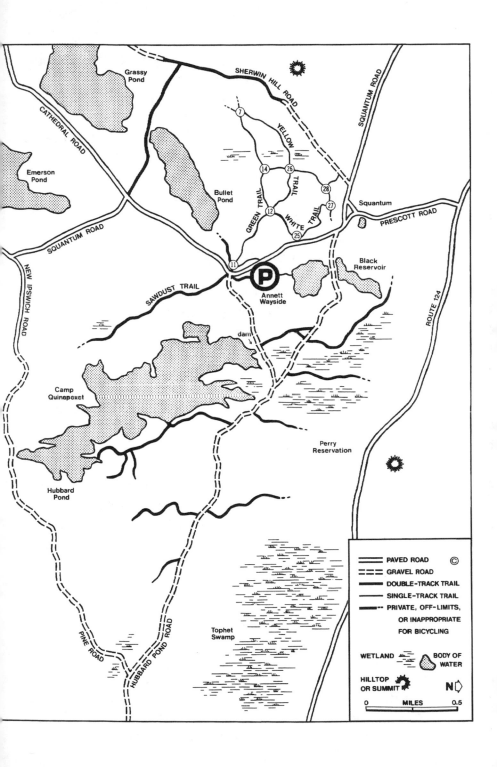

Grassy Pond

CATHEDRAL ROAD

Emerson Pond

SHERWIN HILL ROAD

SQUANTUM ROAD

⑦

YELLOW TRAIL

Bullet Pond

⑭ ㉖

GREEN TRAIL

⑫

WHITE TRAIL

㉘

㉗

Squantum

PRESCOTT ROAD

SQUANTUM ROAD

㉕

NEW IPSWICH ROAD

⑪

P

Annett Wayside

SAWDUST TRAIL

Black Reservoir

ROUTE 124

dam

Camp Quinapoxet

Perry Reservation

Hubbard Pond

PINE ROAD

HUBBARD POND ROAD

Tophet Swamp

PAVED ROAD   ©
GRAVEL ROAD
DOUBLE-TRACK TRAIL
SINGLE-TRACK TRAIL
PRIVATE, OFF-LIMITS,
   OR INAPPROPRIATE
   FOR BICYCLING

WETLAND   BODY OF
                 WATER

HILLTOP
OR SUMMIT   N

0   MILES   0.5

located south of Hubbard Pond.

A 7-mile loop can be made on the back roads around Hubbard Pond. Ride Hubbard Pond Road to where it becomes a maintained, gravel road in the town of New Ipswich and look for **Pine Road** after a half-mile. Descending on the right, Pine Road skirts several wetlands before returning to Rindge, where it is known as **New Ipswich Road**. It rises and falls with a series of low hills, passing a scattering of homes and small ponds along the way. Pavement appears after 2 miles and makes the last half-mile to **Squantum Road** a smooth ride. Turn right to climb back to Cathedral Road, one mile from Annett Wayside.

An obscure road continues across Cathedral Road from this point. Classified as a Class VI road, meaning that it is no longer maintained for regular use, it dips to the shoreline of **Bullet Pond** which is water supply for the neighboring town of Jaffrey. The surrounding property is clearly posted with signs stating that swimming and polluting the land are forbidden. Turn right at the end and follow the stone walls of **Sherwin Hill Road**, another of the area's Class VI roads, over a hilltop where farm fields allow a slight view. Although trees encroach along the sides and decades have passed since it was maintained for regular use, this old road remains a public way. It then descends over a coarse finish of stones to **Squantum Road** in Jaffrey, near the village of **Squantum**. At the bottom, blue tree blazes marking the state forest boundary are visible on one side of the road and a sign for the Beulah Land, another parcel owned by the Society for the Preservation of New Hampshire Forests, sits on the other.

The portion of Annett State Forest lying between Sherwin Hill Road and Cathedral Road contains a great network of single-track trails with intermediate riding. Navigating on these trails is made easy thanks to color-coded markers and intersection numbers, an amenity provided by the nearby Woodbound Inn which grooms the trails for cross country skiing in winter. Shaded by tall hemlock trees and silky smooth from rock-free soils, these paths are a joy to ride. The **Green Trail** leaves Intersection 11 on a flat, easy course which winds through the woods, then descends to Intersection 14 and a difficult swamp crossing. Similarly, the **Yellow Trail** drops from Intersection 12 to cross the same swamp and then proceeds over a rough-cut course of stumps and logs to Intersection 7, near the forest boundary. For a spirited ride try the **White Trail**, which bobs and twists in an exciting series of quick hills and transitions. Be aware that this network of trails continues beyond the state land at several points onto private property.

Driving Directions:
From the center of Jaffrey drive east on Route 124 for 2.2 miles and turn right on Prescott Road at a sign for the Annett Picnic Area. After less than a mile Prescott Road merges at a small village with Squantum Road to become Cathedral Road, and the Wayside Park is less than a half-mile ahead on the left.

From Route 119 in Rindge, Cathedral Road is identified by signs for both Cathedral of the Pines and Annett State Forest. Follow the road north and the Wayside is 2.5 miles ahead on the right. Park beside the road if the gate is locked.

Bike Shops:
Happy Day Cycle, 237 South St., Milford, (603) 673-5088
Spokes & Slopes, 109 Grove St., Peterborough, (603) 924-9961, Rentals Available

USGS Maps:
Peterborough Quadrangle

Additional Information:
New Hampshire Department of Resources and Economic Development, Division of Forests and Lands, P.O. Box 856, Concord, NH 03301-0856, Tel. (603) 271-3457

3
Back Roads
Mason

Separated from the outside world by its quiet hills and dirt roads, the small town of Mason remains a surprisingly unknown place. Only a few minutes drive from the hustle and bustle of Milford and Nashua, and only a few miles from the Massachusetts border, it enjoys a remoteness usually reserved for the more distant parts of the state. Mountain bicyclists can find many great rides throughout the area, from the smoothest gravel to the roughest trail.

While the routes described are public roads and open to recreational uses, some have Class VI designation and are no longer maintained for regular travel. These old roads are obscure from their lack of use and appear to be little more than overgrown trails. Since the surrounding lands are privately owned, visitors are urged to respect the concerns of local residents and minimize their impact.

Begin at **Pratt Pond**, a place where fishermen troll for bass and picnickers feast their eyes on a pristine shoreline. A small parking lot makes this a natural starting point for a mountain bike ride and good routes depart in all directions. The protected woodlands of **Russell-Abbott State Forest** surround the pond and contain several miles of trails, but bicyclists should avoid the short footpath along the northern shoreline because it traverses steep ledges. It eventually terminates at the **millsite** off **Starch Mill Road**. Massive stone walls are the only remains to this intriguing piece of history, which dates from the early 1800's. The mill was the first of its kind and built under great secrecy as a means of processing potatoes to extract starch, a valuable commodity for smoothing and stiffening cloth. Take a few minutes to examine the beautifully constructed, 5-foot-thick walls of the potato storage room, now a peculiar relic of the operation and shaded by full-grown trees. They were necessary to keep the potatoes cool and preserved until processing.

An unnamed woods road begins downhill from this site on Starch Mill Road, and bends for 1.5 miles through pine forest. The route is accessible to off-road vehicles and as a result suffers from ruts and erosion in places, and a population of beavers has dammed several streams along the way leaving some sections under shallow water. These obstacles aside, it is an enjoyable ride in gentle terrain.

The **abandoned railroad bed** holds the easiest biking and best sight-seeing. With rails and ties removed, the grade has a smooth, gravelly surface and stretches for miles past an interesting scenery of ponds, marshes, hillsides, and quarries. Its flatness ensures an effortless means of enjoying these natural surroundings. Although now obscure, this railroad was the lifeblood of surrounding communities in the 1800's when it linked local farming and industry to distant markets. Biking along the grade today allows an appreciation for the work invested in its creation, with large amounts of filling and blasting required for the level passageway. The most costly element of the railway can be seen at its present western terminus above the **Souhegan River**, where a 600-foot stone bridge once spanned the valley at the height of 100 feet. Today the towering stone pillars which remain are an intriguing sight from the end of the embankment. It is a 3-mile ride from Pratt Pond to this outlook, not far beyond Adams Hill Road.

Good bicycling on the railroad bed stretches for a longer distance in the opposite direction where the corridor turns gradually southward to Massachusetts. Signs of granite quarrying are evident along this portion, and easily seen on the hillside where the railroad bed intersects the high-voltage power lines near Starch Mill Road. Granite was an important export for Mason in the late 1800's and was used in buildings, statues, and monuments across the country. Spurs connect to several other quarries but are

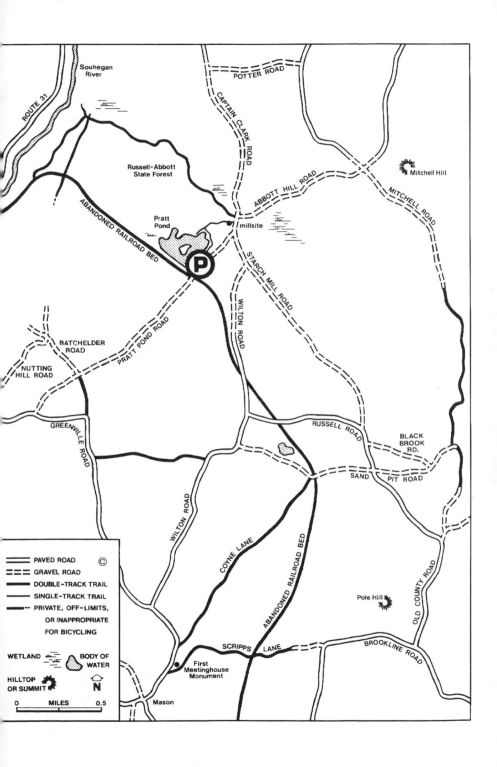

Souhegan
River

ROUTE 31

POTTER ROAD

CAPTAIN CLARK ROAD

Russell-Abbott
State Forest

ABANDONED RAILROAD BED

ABBOTT HILL ROAD

MITCHELL ROAD

Mitchell Hill

Pratt
Pond

millsite

STARCH MILL ROAD

WILTON ROAD

PRATT POND ROAD

BATCHELDER
ROAD

NUTTING
HILL ROAD

GREENVILLE ROAD

RUSSELL ROAD

BLACK
BROOK
RD.

SAND   PIT ROAD

WILTON ROAD

COYNE LANE

ABANDONED RAILROAD BED

OLD COUNTY ROAD

Pole Hill

PAVED ROAD   ©
GRAVEL ROAD
DOUBLE-TRACK TRAIL
SINGLE-TRACK TRAIL
PRIVATE, OFF-LIMITS,
   OR INAPPROPRIATE
   FOR BICYCLING

WETLAND   BODY OF
                 WATER

HILLTOP
OR SUMMIT   N

0   MILES   0.5

SCRIPPS LANE

BROOKLINE ROAD

First
Meetinghouse
Monument

Mason

posted with *No Trespassing* signs. Continuing to the south, the riding is eventually obstructed by rails and ties which remain embedded in the ground.

Mason's gravel roads and Class VI roads offer many more mountain biking routes. After several hundred years of use these roads remain free of both pavement and traffic, and link the old houses and small farms of the area as they wind through rounded hills. **Pratt Pond Road** is an especially pretty ride as it rises for 1.2 miles from the pond to **Greenville Road** with barely a sign of civilization, arcing past exposed ledge and abundant mountain laurel bushes. Unbroken forest gives it the feel of a backcountry road.

Across from **Batchelder Road** an unnamed Class VI road takes a direct route up to Greenville Road, which turns sharply to the south and crosses an open area of fields and distant views. A half-mile past **Wilton Road** look for two Class VI roads intersecting on the left near the **First Meetinghouse Monument**. The timeless village of **Mason** sits just beyond this point. **Coyne Lane** is the more rideable of these old roads, and takes a rolling course to the railroad bed and **Sand Pit Road**. Mountain laurel bushes thrive in the Mason area and form a distinctive evergreen border along this road. **Scripps Lane** is badly eroded and a more difficult ride as it descends abruptly to the abandoned railroad bed. Pratt Pond Road, Greenville Road, Coyne Lane, and the railroad bed form a 7-mile ride from Pratt Pond.

Starch Mill Road lies in flatter terrain and stetches for 1.5 miles between the base of **Abbott Hill Road** and the pavement of **Russell Road**. To complete a 5.5-mile loop, turn left on **Black Brook Road**, then left on Sand Pit Road. At the end turn left on **Mitchell Road**, a Class VI road which appears as a faint wagon track leading across a small field below a farmhouse. Do not confuse Mitchell Road with the driveway to this house, which is bordered by stone walls. A difficult ride in places, the old road drops to a brook which must be waded, passes the remains of a mill, intersects the powerlines, and emerges on smooth gravel after 1.3 miles. It then continues for another mile over a hill to Abbott Hill Road. Turn left and coast for 1 mile back to Starch Mill Road to complete the ride.

Driving Directions:
From Route 101 between Milford and Peterborough, turn south on Route 31 and then immediately left on Isaac Frye Highway. Cross a bridge over the Souhegan River and turn right on Captain Clark Road, which becomes Starch Mill Road when it crosses from Wilton to Mason. After 2.5 miles turn right on Pratt Pond Road and find parking beside the pond, a half-mile ahead.

From Route 119 in Massachusetts, turn north on Canal Street at West Townsend, drive for 1.3 miles and bear right on Mason Road. Continue for 4 miles to the center of Mason, then turn right on Meetinghouse Hill Road and follow it for a mile. Bear left at the fork on Greenville Road and after 1.7 miles turn right on Pratt Pond Road. Parking at the pond is 1.2 miles ahead on the left.

Bike Shops:
Happy Day Cycle, 237 South St., Milford, (603) 673-5088

USGS Maps:
Peterborough Quadrangle

4
Mine Falls Park
Nashua

    Mine Falls Park is home to all kinds of activities, from organized team sports to solitary strolls through the woods. Fishermen appear to outnumber the fish on some days, joggers crisscross the area's trails, and bicyclists roll by with ease. Impressively, the park manages to satisfy this demand and accommodates vast numbers of visitors on sunny weekends while generously sharing its quiet pine forests and pleasant water views. An oasis in a sprawling city, Mine Falls Park is a narrow strip of only 325 acres but harbors a dense network of trails ranging from paved bicycle routes to narrow footpaths. It is an ideal place to escape the confines of civilization and a wonderful surprise for first-time visitors.

    Owned by the city, Mine Falls Park has been a natural for Nashua's off-road bicyclists but its proximity mandates that riders tread lightly. Not the place for high speeds or long tours, the park's small area and populated setting require that bicyclists be extra cautious in their trail manners. The place is alive with walkers, runners, and other riders, so be particularly sensitive to concerns of safety and erosion.

    Big hills are nonexistent at Mine Falls, which makes many of these trails perfect for beginners and lifelong flatlanders. Most routes are broad, obstacle-free, and suitable for any ability, with sandy soils making the riding exceptionally smooth. Tree roots and tight spaces interfere on a handful of single-track trails, providing good options for intermediate and advanced riders. Wherever you pedal, the park's well-kept condition and thoughtful planning will be apparent. Signs are stationed at many trail intersections to display directions and distances (in kilometers) to various destinations. Pedestrian bridges and underpasses have been built to allow the trails to cross the various waterways and roads encountered. And the trails link distant neighborhoods to provide direct access for many local residents.

Spine Road is appropriately the backbone to the park's network of options, and divides the strip of land between the **Nashua River** and the **Nashua Canal**. Several miles in length, the gravel road is firm and smooth and will welcome even the most timid mountain bicyclist with easy pedaling in the shade of evergreen forest. Gradually sloped in some areas, it descends with the river and the canal from west to east. An underpass allows it to travel beneath the **Everett Turnpike**, linking two otherwise separate halves of the park.

A second woods road branches from Spine Road near its western endpoint and traces the northern shore of **Mill Pond**, where pleasant views stretch over the water. The route follows the shoreline as the pond narrows into the canal and then arcs gently beside the waterway to rejoin Spine Road. This makes an equally easygoing alternative to Spine Road and the two routes combine to form a 2-mile loop.

A similarly easy, 2-mile ride can be made on the eastern end of Spine Road where a variety of interesting sights can be viewed. Begin at the park's main entrance at the end of **Whipple Street**, cross the footbridge over the canal and turn right, following the path along the grassy bank of the waterway as it curves with a gentle flow. The trail passes a pretty view over **the Cove**, once a sharp bend in the Nashua River and now a self-contained deadwater. It then meets a gate at the outskirts of the **Millyard**, a collection of old mill buildings which were once the focal point of Nashua's industrial success. They now house a variety of small businesses. Continue along the driveway to an intersection with Spine Road, evident as a dirt road

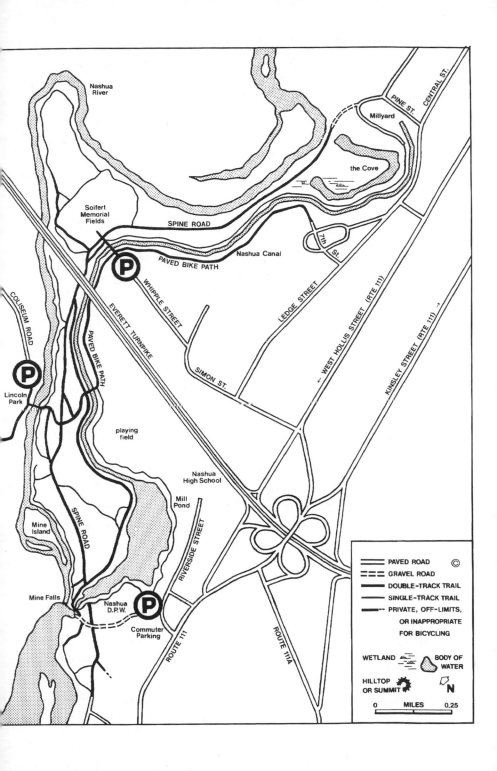

Nashua River

Millyard

PINE ST.

CENTRAL ST.

the Cove

Soifert
Memorial
Fields

SPINE ROAD

7th St.

Nashua Canal

PAVED BIKE PATH

P

COLISEUM ROAD

WHIPPLE STREET

EVERETT TURNPIKE

PAVED BIKE PATH

LEDGE STREET

WEST HOLLIS STREET (RTE 111)

KINSLEY STREET (RTE 111)

SIMON ST.

P

Lincoln
Park

playing
field

Nashua
High School

Mill
Pond

Mine
Island

SPINE ROAD

RIVERSIDE STREET

Mine Falls

Nashua
D.P.W.

P

Commuter
Parking

ROUTE 111

ROUTE 111A

PAVED ROAD   ©
GRAVEL ROAD
DOUBLE-TRACK TRAIL
SINGLE-TRACK TRAIL
PRIVATE, OFF-LIMITS,
   OR INAPPROPRIATE
   FOR BICYCLING

WETLAND   BODY OF
                        WATER

HILLTOP
OR SUMMIT   N

0   MILES   0.25

descending on the left toward the river, and return gradually uphill to the footbridge at Whipple Street, a mile away. The canal's earthen banks can be seen to rise 30 feet above this stretch of Spine Road.

The **Paved Bike Path** presents one of the most civilized forms of off-road riding. Far removed from the city's busy streets, the route offers bicyclists effortless rolling over smooth pavement in the peace and quiet of a car-free environment. The bike path makes an enjoyable, 2-mile cruise from one end to the other and is surrounded by trees, water, and all the elements of nature. It stretches from **Lincoln Park** at the end of **Coliseum Road** to **7th Street**, following the canal for most of the way. Bridges allow it to pass over both the river and the canal, and beneath the Everett Turnpike.

Highly recommended for more adept riders is the single-track loop extending north from the **Soifert Memorial Fields** on a peninsula of land created by a hairpin turn in the river. The smooth, narrow course frolics at the water's edge, weaving with a constant flow of trees and small bumps. It is a 1.5-mile trip and, although the western end of the trail suffers from the traffic noise of the highway, much of the riding holds a surprisingly isolated flavor.

Similar riding can be found upstream. The single-track stretching from the **Commuter Parking** area on **Riverside Street** past the **Nashua High School** is an engaging ride requiring precise bicycling skills. It is a narrow path along the southern shore of Mill Pond with an exciting roller coaster of small hills. From the footbridge at Lincoln Park, narrow paths extend in both directions along the river as it bends beneath overhanging trees. These trails weave through the woods, bump over logs, and roll with quick ups and downs. The river's peaceful scenery is easily admired at points along the way. The path opposite **Mine Island** is an especially difficult ride as bicyclists are squeezed by a steep slope and distracted by the roar of the river below.

A dam sits above the rugged ledges of **Mine Falls**, where the water flows through a chasm in a spectacle seldom found in the flatlands of southern New Hampshire. Named for a nearby lead mine, the falls began fueling Nashua's industrial boom in 1824 when the Nashua Manufacturing Company purchased the surrounding land to build the dam and canal. Although the mills have long since closed, the dam remains intact and now harnesses the river's energy for the generation of electricity, while also providing a vast area of open water for fishing and boating.

Driving Directions:
To reach parking at Whipple Street take Exit 5 from the Everett Turnpike and drive for a half-mile east on Route 111 (Kinsley Street), a one-way road. Turn left at signs for Route 111 west and reverse direction (West Hollis Street), then turn right on Simon Street. Whipple Street is a half-mile ahead.

For the commuter parking lot on Riverside Street head west from Exit 5 on Route 111 and turn right at the sign for commuter parking on Panther Drive. Continue to the end and the parking area is directly across Riverside Street.

Lincoln Park is accessed from Exit 6. Take Broad Street west past the Nashua Mall and turn left on Coliseum Road. The trailhead is at the end of the road.

Bike Shops:
Goodale's Bike & Ski, 46 Main St., Nashua, (603) 882-2111
Hetzer's Bicycle Shop, 5 Lowell Rd., Hudson, (603) 882-5566
Tony's Bicycle Shop, 433 Amherst St., Nashua, (603) 886-5912

USGS Maps:
Nashua North Quadrangle

Additional Information:
Nashua Conservation Commission, Nashua City Hall, 229 Main Street, Nashua, NH 03061

5
Massabesic Lake
Auburn

Only four miles from downtown Manchester, Massabesic Lake is a wonderful retreat from the hustle of the nearby city. Known for its easy riding and peaceful terrain, the area is ideal for bicycling and offers an unending supply of mellow woods roads, complete with quiet forests and water views. Trails are found in a variety of locations around the lake, providing a different ride for each day of the week and many options for longer tours.

Massabesic is a Native American word meaning *place of much water*, a point not lost by the city of Manchester which has used the 2500-acre lake as a water supply since the 1870's. The lake and its 32 miles of shoreline have attracted visitors since the 1800's when summer tourists came from Boston for the clean air and inspiring natural scenery, as well as the free-spirited nightlife at nearby saloons and dance halls. Today the pristine shoreline serves as a popular backdrop for sailing and boating, as well as fishing for plentiful bass, perch, and pickerel. Hikers ramble miles of quiet trails to find secluded coves, some with sandy beaches. And bicyclists can leave the surrounding pavement and roll along miles of smooth woods roads with ease, enjoying the sounds of waves lapping at the shore as they ride.

Because **Massabesic Lake** is a water supply important rules apply to use of the area. These regulations are posted at most trailheads and enforced by the staff of the **Manchester Water Works**, who patrol the trails regularly. Swimming or wading anywhere in the lake is strictly forbidden. In addition, several areas of the property are off-limits to the public because they are in proximity to the pumping station's water intake pipe, where strong currents exist. *No Wheeled Vehicles* signs are posted at all trailheads but apply only to motorized use, so bicycling and other passive uses are permitted. Posted because of concerns of erosion, these signs are a reminder to bicyclists to pedal softly and to never ride when conditions are wet. The Water Works also asks that visitors be careful not to block trailhead gates when parking so that emergency vehicles and other work crews always have access.

Given the area's large scale and abundance of nameless trails, visitors are advised to bring a map along when exploring for the first time. Fortunately, the lake itself is a dominant natural feature for easy orientation. Massabesic's trails are separated into several distinct areas, but each can be linked for longer tours with minimal amounts of road riding. The distance by road around the eastern part of the lake totals 10 miles. Wherever you decide to ride, pick your route carefully on windy days because the lake's large, open area leaves some trails exposed.

Stretching across the entire trail system, the **abandoned railroad bed** connects **Lake Shore Road** to **Chester Turnpike**. It was built in the 1860's to connect Manchester's burgeoning mills to the seaport of Portsmouth, and stopped at Auburn's depot on the southern end of **Clark Pond** to load lumber and ice, the town's primary exports. With its rails and ties removed, the grade is now a popular recreation trail and an effortless way to enjoy the area's natural scenery. The gravel surface is both free of obstacles and well-drained. Bridges cross the many streams encountered and a tunnel allows the trail to pass beneath **Hooksett Road**. Identifiable by metal gates at road crossings and a distinctly straight and level course, the abandoned railroad bed passes the main parking area by the **Candia Road** traffic circle.

Deer Neck extends southward from this point, dividing Massabesic into two large halves which are connected only by a narrow channel. Much of Deer Neck is privately owned but good biking routes follow both the southern and eastern shores, where there are nice views of the lake from places like **Rocky Point**. Bicyclists will encounter a few hills but most of the trails are easy riding. Note that the northern terminus of the **Fire Point Trail** is also a driveway, so be respectful of nearby residences.

Parking is also available at **Deer Neck Bridge**, where more trails depart from both sides of **Bypass Route 28**. Pedaling **Battery Point Trail** out to **Battery Point** is an easy 1-mile trip along a smooth woods road and rewards visitors with a panoramic view of the lake. Surrounded by water, the point can also be vulnerable to the wind on some days. Two short sections of nearby single-track offer a challenging combination of tight corners and constant hurdles, while a series of double-tracks running southward remain free of obstacles. **Deerneck Road** and **Spofford Road** connect to **Canfield Cove**, where bicyclists can find more options for trail riding including the popular **Coffin Point Trail** which skirts the shoreline to **Route 121**.

Nearby, 580-foot **Mine Hill** presents ambitious riders with a climb of 330 feet over the course of a half-mile. Also known as Devil's Den Hill after a reputed cave in its side, the slope makes for an unrelenting, heart-pounding ascent. The trail is double-track all the way to the top and mostly free of obstacles. A lookout tower which once stood at the summit is now gone, but a view of the surrounding hills can be had once the leaves have fallen.

A better vista can be enjoyed from the **ledges** topping the ridgeline north of the lake where the horizon stretches across the Merrimack River Valley. Reached after a short ride over difficult single-track, the ledges crown a hilly area of intermediate woods roads like **Currier Point Trail** and **Upper Currier Point Trail**.

Another network of trails and old roads lies beyond **Bunker Hill** on **Dearborn Road**. An unnamed double-track loops around a small mill pond for a trouble-free ride but its

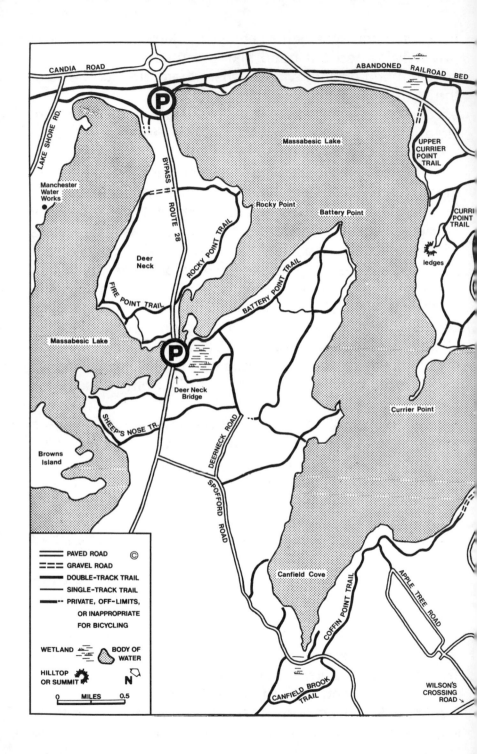

proximity to Bunker Hill creates some ups and downs. In this area Chester Turnpike degrades to a rough jeep road which is perfect for fat-tire riding, as are nearby **Gospel Path** and **Birch Road**. Though they extend beyond the Manchester Water Works land, these roads remain public property. **Bunker Hill Road**, **Eaton Road**, and Chester Turnpike are quiet, country streets linking the area.

Some of the easiest riding is found on the shores of **Little Massabesic Lake**, located just beyond **Auburn center**. Here flat terrain and smooth, well-graded forest roads meander through acres of quiet woods, making it the perfect place for a first-time experience. A variety of evergreen forests, including red pine, white pine, and hemlock, give a different feel to various places along these trails. Many of the forests were planted during the Great Depression to control both erosion and evaporation in Massabesic's watershed. Bordered by an expanse of wetlands, the lake adds to the interesting scenery, especially from the shoreline routes off **Raymond Road** where a peninsula provides a nice picnicking spot. Beginning from the parking lot on **Depot Road**, bicyclists can make a 3-mile loop around the lake using easy trails and the gravel surface of Raymond Road. South of Raymond Road a more challenging trail climbs along a hill only to reach private land at the top.

North of the abandoned railroad bed and Depot Road lies Clark Pond, a long, narrow body of water along the course of Maple Falls Brook. It is possible to circle the pond on a variety of trails and to continue across Candia Road and Route 101 to Tower Hill Pond, another popular area for mountain biking and the subject of the next chapter.

Driving Directions:

From Interstate 93 take Exit 7 and follow Route 101 east, then take Exit 1 for Bypass Route 28 south. Park at the lot near the Candia Road traffic circle or continue for another mile to Deer Neck Channel.

To reach the parking area on Depot Road, take Exit 2 from Route 101 and turn south on Hooksett Road, toward Auburn. After 0.8 miles turn left on Depot Road and park at the turnout 0.2 miles ahead. Only the major parking areas are shown on the map and limited parking is available at many other trailheads.

Bike Shops:

All Outdoors, 321 Elm St., Manchester, (603) 624-1468

Banagan's Cycling Company, 4 Vinton St., Manchester, (603) 623-3330

Bike Barn, 255 Maple St., Manchester, (603) 668-6555

Don's Family Sports Center, 1158 Hooksett Rd., Hooksett, (603) 644-5464

Haggett's Bicycle Shop, 920 Second St., Manchester, (603) 624-8362

Nault's, 30-32 Bridge St., Manchester, (603) 669-7993

USGS Maps:

Manchester North Quadrangle, Candia Quadrangle, Manchester South Quadrangle, Derry Quadrangle

Additional Information:

Manchester Water Works, 281 Lincoln Street, Manchester, NH 03103

6
Tower Hill Pond
Candia

Cupped in a small valley, Tower Hill Pond enjoys a solitude unique to places so close to civilization. A ring of hills isolates this neighborhood of trails from the outside world and an expanse of open water highlights the area's natural beauty. Adjoining the massive trail network at Massabesic Lake, the 10 miles of woods roads at Tower Hill Pond are another welcome retreat only miles from Manchester, and contain both leisurely shoreline rides and challenging hill climbs.

Managed by the Manchester Water Works as part of the Massabesic Lake watershed, **Tower Hill Pond** is a public water supply so certain rules apply to use of the area. A list of regulations is posted at the main trailhead, and wading and swimming are among the forbidden activities. As with most areas, use is restricted to daylight hours, fires are prohibited, and visitors are expected to carry out what they carry in. Signs reading *No Wheeled Vehicles* apply only to motorized vehicles, and bicycles are permitted on the property. The Water Works staff also advises trail users not to block the trailhead gates when parking, since work crews and emergency vehicles need access at all times.

There are no signs to guide the visitor on the trails at Tower Hill Pond and no trail names have been designated, which makes navigating through the network more difficult. Fortunately, it is possible to use dominant natural features like the pond and surrounding elevations, as well as the flow of Maple Falls Brook which bisects the area. If you are unfamiliar with the trails, bring the map along and be conscious of your course.

The main access trail from **Tower Hill Road** arrives

near two **dams** built to contain the pond. Once paved, the road has crumbled away to leave a gravelly surface extending on a 3-mile loop along the shoreline. The pedaling remains easy and the level grade, gentle hills, and pretty views over the water make it a pleasant trip. In a few places loose stones have been left from erosion, but these pose minor problems.

The shoreline loop can be extended with a variety of surrounding trails. At the southern end of the pond, below the dams, a grassy woods road meanders past a combination of glacial boulders and beaver ponds to form a short and easy loop. Obscured by encroaching tree limbs, two double-track trails lead southward to dead end beside the roar of **Route 101**. For longer tours take Tower Hill Road beneath Route 101, cross **Candia Road**, and look for trails on both sides of **Clark Pond**. They lead southward to miles of possibilities surrounding Massabesic Lake, the subject of the previous chapter.

A difficult ride can be had on the trail leading up the hill from the western side of the pond. After a tough climb on a single-track trail spiced with rocks and logs, the route becomes bogged by several mudholes before continuing onto private property. This boundary is marked by blue tree blazes.

The northern end of the pond holds additional ups and downs with double-track width. Though loose rock and steep hills challenge bicyclists in a few spots, the riding is generally intermediate and a 2-mile loop can be made between New Hampshire **Snowmobile Corridor Trail 15** and Maple Falls Brook. The trail explores interesting scenery as it winds among the rocky hills above the pond and descends along the course of Maple Falls Brook back to the shoreline. A grassy trail short-cuts this loop to avoid most of the hill climbing.

The trail to **Maple Falls** is also an intermediate ride, not for its obstacles but for its hills. A carry is required to cross the brook, which races through the slueceway of an old **millsite**.

50

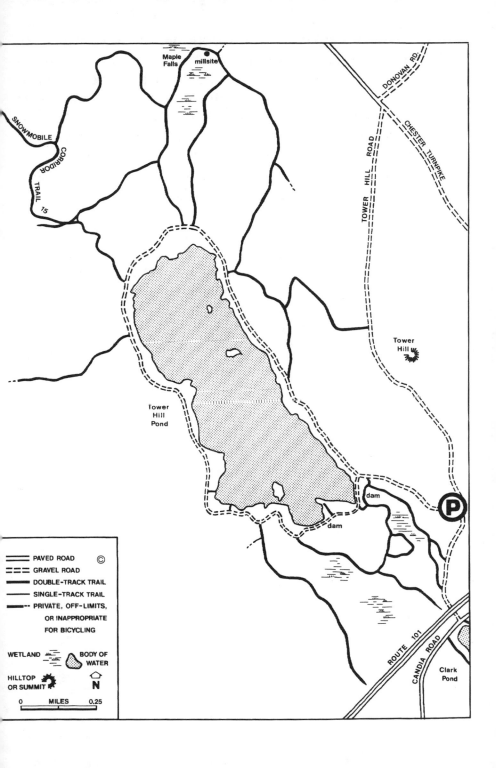

Maple
Falls   millsite

SNOWMOBILE

CORRIDOR

TRAIL 15

DONOVAN RD.

CHESTER TURNPIKE

TOWER HILL ROAD

Tower
Hill

Tower
Hill
Pond

P

dam

dam

PAVED ROAD ©
GRAVEL ROAD
DOUBLE-TRACK TRAIL
SINGLE-TRACK TRAIL
PRIVATE, OFF-LIMITS,
OR INAPPROPRIATE
FOR BICYCLING

WETLAND   BODY OF
               WATER

HILLTOP
OR SUMMIT   N

0   MILES   0.25

ROUTE 101

CANDIA ROAD

Clark
Pond

Plainly evident from the opposite shore of the pond, the radio tower crowning **Tower Hill** marks the area's highest point. A rough jeep trail tackles the slope, gaining 300' in elevation from the water's edge. The incline is persistant and after a switchback it finally moderates at a stand of red pine. As with other stands in the Massabesic watershed, these trees were planted as part of the forest management program which began during the Great Depression. The trail terminates at Tower Hill Road, just shy of the top.

Turn right and follow the road south to return to the main trailhead, about a half-mile down hill, or turn left and coast down the opposite side for more riding. Tower Hill Road terminates at **Chester Turnpike**, which takes a long, straight course between the towns of Chester and Allenstown, some 12 miles apart. Though several sections of the road are paved and quite civilized, others remain primitive. Nearby **Donovan Road** starts with easy riding then degrades to trail before being halted by a washed-out bridge.

Driving Directions:

From Interstate 93 take Exit 7 for Route 101 East, then Exit 2 for Hooksett Road. Turn south on Hooksett Road and continue toward Auburn center for only 0.2 miles, then turn left on Candia Road. Drive for a half-mile to where the road crosses Maple Falls Brook beside a pond, and look for Tower Hill Road on the left. Unmarked and unpaved, the road passes beneath a concrete bridge on Route 101 and climbs Tower Hill to join the trails on the left. Roadside parking exists at the trailheads, but remember not to block the gates when parking.

Bike Shops:

All Outdoors, 321 Elm St., Manchester, (603) 624-1468

Banagan's Cycling Company, 4 Vinton St., Manchester, (603) 623-3330

Bike Barn, 255 Maple St., Manchester, (603) 668-6555

Don's Family Sports Center, 1158 Hooksett Rd., Hooksett, (603) 644-5464

Haggett's Bicycle Shop, 920 Second St., Manchester, (603) 624-8362

Nault's, 30-32 Bridge St., Manchester, (603) 669-7993

USGS Maps:

Manchester North Quadrangle, Candia Quadrangle

Additional Information:

Manchester Water Works, 281 Lincoln Street, Manchester, NH 03103

7
Pawtuckaway State Park
Nottingham

Conveniently positioned between Manchester, Concord, and Portsmouth, Pawtuckaway State Park ranks as one of southern New Hampshire's greatest trail resources. Its name is a Native American word meaning *the place of the big buck*, and today the area's impressive views and prized natural features continue to reward visitors. Three mountains dominate the park with views extending from the Atlantic Ocean to the White Mountains, and a combination of easy gravel roads and challenging foot trails penetrates 5,500 acres of quiet woodlands. Bicyclists can enjoy seeing scenic beaver ponds, huge glacial boulders, and several historical relics as they ride.

Read trailhead notices before riding at Pawtuckaway, since mountain biking is not permitted on all trails. The park manager stresses that erosion has become a concern and that riders should do their best to minimize impact. Riding off trails or in wet conditions is prohibited. Volunteer trail maintenance projects are planned to restore some routes and interested cyclists are urged to help. The park's multi-use trails are enjoyed by hikers, equestrians, and even vehicles in some places, so ride with care.

Pawtuckaway can be accessed at several points. The main entrance is located off **Mountain Road** at the southern boundary and is open between mid-May and mid-October, when a small admission fee is charged. A large parking lot located outside the gate accommodates visitors in the off-season. This entrance is busy on summer weekends when thousands come to enjoy **Pawtuckaway Pond** and perhaps spend the night at the **campground**, where 160 sites are available on a first-come, first-served basis.   Others come to enjoy the park's **beach** or take a stroll along the nearby trails.   Bicyclists arriving at the main entrance should expect to encounter traffic on **State Park Road** during summer, and are advised by the park staff to be extra cautious on adjoining trails.   Other points of access include the **Fundy Boat Launch** off **Deerfield Road** on the northern perimeter and **Reservation Road** in the mountainous area to the west.

The **Fundy Trail** is one of Pawtuckaway's friendliest, as gentle hills and ample width ease the 1.5-mile ride from State Park Road to Fundy Boat Launch.   The trail begins about 1.5 miles from the entrance gate.   Although a few rocks and tree roots pepper the surface, the open scenery of **Burnham's Marsh** and **Fundy Cove** make it a very enjoyable ride and several side trails explore outlooks over the water.   The trail extending eastward from the boat ramp along the cove is New Hampshire Snowmobile Corridor Trail 17, which eventually continues beyond the park boundary onto private lands.   Another snowmobile trail leaves from the boat launch in the opposite direction and gives a challenging ride over bumps and puddles before dead-ending.

The **Shaw Trail** is off-limits to bicycles. Conditions on the 3-mile route between Fundy Trail and **Tower Road** have deteriorated and park officials believe that the many wet spots and steep ups and downs are inappropriate for bicycling. Some areas are even flooded during periods of high water. At publication, a new trail for bikes is proposed between these two areas but until it is completed mountain bikers will have to use surrounding routes.

The intermediate riding conditions of **Mountain Trail** and **Round Pond Trail** offer an alternative means of connecting the east and west ends of the park.   The 2-mile Mountain Trail leaves the road at the shore of **Mountain Pond**, a half-mile below the entrance gate, and climbs a long hill before intersecting Round Pond Trail.   This first stretch of riding is relatively easy, but Mountain Trail becomes more challenging as the surface degrades and the hills get bigger, especially near **South Mountain**. Erosion has become a concern on Mountain Trail, so pedal softly and keep in mind that it could one day be closed to bicycles. Round Pond Trail takes an intermediate route to the same general area by following the stone walls of an old wagon road to the end of Reservation Road. Well-conditioned riders can combine the Fundy, Shaw, and Mountain Trails with State Park Road and Tower Road for an 8-mile loop.

The western half of the park contains a collection of jeep roads which provide miles of easy riding. Dividing three mountain ridges, these gravel roads originated in the 1800's when they were used by the area's small farms, now evident only by cellar holes and small cemeteries. The roads also access some of Pawtuckaway's most intriguing natural features. Similar to Tower Road, **Round Pond Road** is well-drained and navigable by car, although some spots are rough with erosion and require intermediate riding skills. Round Pond Road passes large wetlands before joining with Tower Road to form a 3-mile loop off Reservation Road.

Pack a lunch and descend to scenic **Round Pond**, nestled beneath surrounding hillsides with a picturesque shoreline of coves and ledges. Visit the nearby **Boulder Field** where gigantic pieces of rock came to rest after glaciers broke them from surrounding cliffs thousands of years ago. They represent one of the largest collections of naturally transported boulders to be found anywhere. The largest is 6,000-ton Churchill Rock and measures 60 feet long, 40 feet wide, and 40 feet high. The **Boulder Trail** connects this area to Round Pond Road and is easiest if taken from the western end, since the eastern segment is a challenging single-track sandwiched between the cliffs of Rocky Ridge on one side and a swamp on the other. **Devil's Den** is a short pedal from the boulders, although a steep climb separates the two sites. Leave bicycles at Dead Pond, where the trail becomes unrideable, and scramble up the trail to the cave where a rare, luminescent moss grows on the back wall. Devil's Den is less than a mile from Round

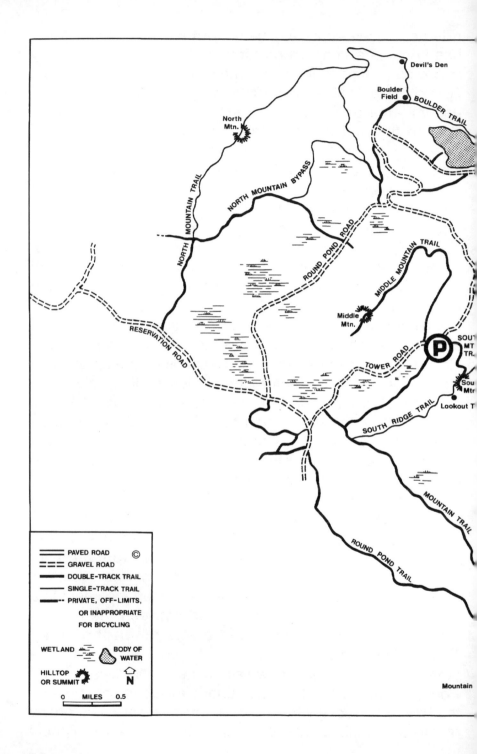

Devil's Den

Boulder
Field

BOULDER TRAIL

North
Mtn.

NORTH MOUNTAIN TRAIL

NORTH MOUNTAIN BYPASS

ROUND POND ROAD

MIDDLE MOUNTAIN TRAIL

Middle
Mtn.

SOUT
MT
TR.

RESERVATION ROAD

TOWER ROAD

Sou
Mtr

Lookout T

SOUTH RIDGE TRAIL

MOUNTAIN TRAIL

ROUND POND TRAIL

PAVED ROAD   ©

GRAVEL ROAD

DOUBLE-TRACK TRAIL

SINGLE-TRACK TRAIL

PRIVATE, OFF-LIMITS,
OR INAPPROPRIATE
FOR BICYCLING

WETLAND   BODY OF
WATER

HILLTOP
OR SUMMIT   N

0   MILES   0.5

Mountain

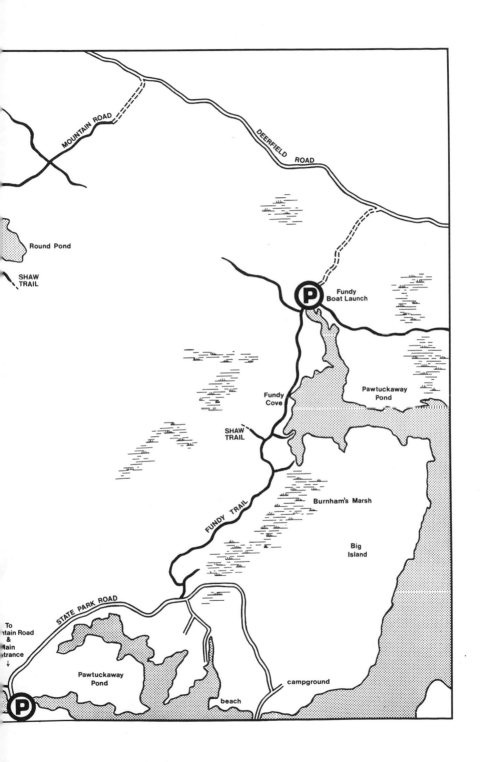

Pond Road via the western end of the Boulder Trail.

The **North Mountain Trail** continues above Devil's Den along the ridge of **North Mountain**, and reaches the summit at 1011 feet elevation with distant views along the way. Unfortunately the steepness and roughness of the trail make much of it unrideable. Far below, the **North Mountain Bypass** takes a more capable route in the shadow of the mountain, beginning as a double-track near Round Pond Road. After climbing to a viewpoint of the mountain's cliff side, the trail descends as a single-track, turns southward, and later merges with an old wagon road. From this point it is an intermediate ride to the North Mountain Trail and Reservation Road.

Trails climbing Pawtuckaway's other mountains are more manageable, but require particular caution since they are popular hiking routes. The mile-long **Middle Mountain Trail** rises gradually beside a stone wall at the base of **Middle Mountain**, then turns and ascends with several steep switchbacks. After a brief hike, bicyclists have an easy ride for the final half-mile along the top of the ridgeline before reaching an open ledge with a great view of surrounding hills and dales.

South Mountain Trail takes a more direct route to a neighboring summit but is generally too steep to ride. The more gradual **South Ridge Trail** is marked by white blazes and ascends through pretty hemlock groves and slabs of exposed ledge, but is a treacherous undertaking and even advanced riders should expect to walk some sections. A **lookout tower** stands at the top of South Mountain and provides a fantastic view on a clear day from the Atlantic Ocean to the White Mountains.

Driving Directions:

From Route 101 take Exit 5 and follow Route 107 north to its intersection with Routes 27 and 156. Turn left, then right at the next intersection, following Route 156 north. After 1.3 miles turn left on Mountain Road at a large state park sign and the park's main entrance is 2 miles ahead on the left.

For the Fundy Boat Launch continue north on Route 156 to Nottingham Square, then turn left on Deerfield Road.

For parking on Tower Road continue on Routes 107 and 27, heading north toward Deerfield. Bear right on Route 107 after it splits with Route 27, and after 3 miles turn right on Reservation Road. Continue for 2.2 miles, turn left at a sign marked *Lookout Tower*, and parking is less than a mile ahead at the base of South Mountain.

Bike Shops:

Exeter Cycles, 32 Portsmouth Ave., Exeter, (603) 778-2331

Stratham Hill Bicycle, 240 Portsmouth Ave., Stratham, (603) 778-8180

Wheel Power Bicycle Shop, 37 Water St., Exeter, (603) 772-6343

USGS Maps:

Mount Pawtuckaway Quadrangle

Additional Information:

Park Manager, Pawtuckaway State Park, 128 Mountain Road, Raymond, NH 03077, Tel. (603) 895-3031

8
Bear Brook State Park
Allenstown

New Hampshire's largest developed park is an ideal place to ride a mountain bike. Bear Brook encompasses nearly 10,000 acres of forests and offers some 30 miles of multi-use trails, and is located only ten miles from both Concord and Manchester. It is a network so vast that you could spend several days exploring and not retrace your tracks. A good mix of trails explores the area's small mountains and pretty ponds, while remote destinations invite day-long tours. Complemented by swimming beaches, a picnic area, campground, fitness course, two summer camps, and even an archery range, Bear Brook State Park is a place for all kinds of outdoor enjoyment.

All trails within the park are open to bicycling unless otherwise posted, but be aware that routes in two areas are closed to the general public during the summer months when youth camps are in session. The gravel roads near Bear Hill Pond Camp and Spruce Pond Camp are both posted for this restriction. Many other trails at Bear Brook are busy with hikers on weekends, so use careful judgement when choosing a route and ride responsibly. Fortunately there have been few problems with mountain biking at the park and it is hoped that the multi-use trail policy will continue to be acceptable to all.

The Park Manager also advises visitors that Bear Brook is a popular place for hunting in the late fall, so bicycling is not a recommended activity during that period. Riders should be attentive to the state park's deceptively large scale, as long distances separate many intersections and some trails stray far into remote areas. Keep track of your energy levels and turn back before you get tired.

Numbered and lettered signs displayed at intersections correspond to those printed on the map, so bring a copy along for easier navigation. An entrance fee is charged during the high season in the spring and summer, and is payable at a toll booth beside **Allenstown-Deerfield Road**.

Bear Brook's gravel roads are wide and well-drained and offer miles of smooth pedaling. **Podunk Road** is the most predominant as it takes a 4-mile course through the center of the park and intersects a vast number of other trails. Stone walls reveal its old age, but some sections have been improved for vehicle traffic. After climbing from the parking lot on a short stretch of pavement, the broad, gravel road passes an open field and small pond, then begins a long climb on the slopes of **Bear Hill**. A small sign marks intersection 7 and **Spruce Pond Road**, which diverges left and descends to the **youth camp** at **Spruce Pond**. Farther ahead a righthand turn at intersection 9 reaches the camp at **Bear Hill Pond**. Remember that during the summer when the camps are in session segments of these side roads are closed to the general public. Podunk Road continues with rougher conditions for another two miles, skirting **Hall Mountain Marsh** before regaining a maintained, gravel finish and emerging at **Currier Road** in the neighboring town of Candia.

Lower Road is a much easier ride since its entire length is paved. It rolls and bends through unbroken forest to **Beaver Pond**, where a **campground** and **beach** are among the state park's most popular attractions. Campsites are available on a first-come, first-served basis. Expect to see cars on Lower Road during the summer season, especially on weekends. For a livelier ride, try the single-track past **Archery Pond** where a relatively smooth surface and an engaging mix of small humps and quick corners keeps bicyclists on their toes. Trails between Lower Road and Podunk Road are designated for cross country skiing in winter, and are distinguished by intersection numbers with the *X-C* prefix. Varying from footpaths to woods roads, these trails have both intermediate and difficult riding. The double-track past **Smith Pond** is flat and easy with tree roots being the only obstacles. A short spur leads to the pond's boggy shores where a lean-to **shelter** provides a good picnicking spot. Across Spruce Pond Road, between intersections X-C 11 and X-C 12, bicyclists have a steady, uphill pedal through a pretty hemlock forest. Expert riders have the option of testing themselves on the trail paralleling Podunk Road between Intersections X-C 12 and X-C 14. Tilted by the slope of Bear Hill, it is a technical ride over jumbles of rocks and several stream crossings.

Circumnavigating Beaver Pond makes a difficult, 2-mile loop. A single-track leaves the beach area with a rocky start and follows the shoreline closely with a mix of wet spots and unrideably steep hills. The narrow path then widens to double-track at a four-way intersection. Turn right and follow the boardwalk across the marsh at the end of the pond to return to the campground, or continue straight to meet the **Hall Mountain Trail**. Riding to Podunk Road is an uphill grind from Beaver Pond with steep pitches and difficult, rocky sections slowing the way. Hall Mountain Trail crosses Podunk Road at an old foundation and ascends a shoulder of **Hall Mountain** with a strenuous climb which skirts the tree-covered summit. It then continues to Intersection 15 with rough, rocky conditions. Given its distance from the parking lot, this ambitious route is recommended only for the fittest riders.

Lots of great biking lies beyond intersection 15, where miles of double-tracks offer rolling hills and loads of solitude. Many of the trails in this area are designated for snowmobiling in winter and are marked and maintained by the local club, the Southern New Hampshire Snow Slickers. Though deeply rutted from off-road vehicle use in places, they enjoy gentle grades and avoidable obstacles. The trail along the northwest shore of Bear Hill Pond has a pretty view over the water and links Podunk Road for an intermediate ride. Just before the trail begins a steep

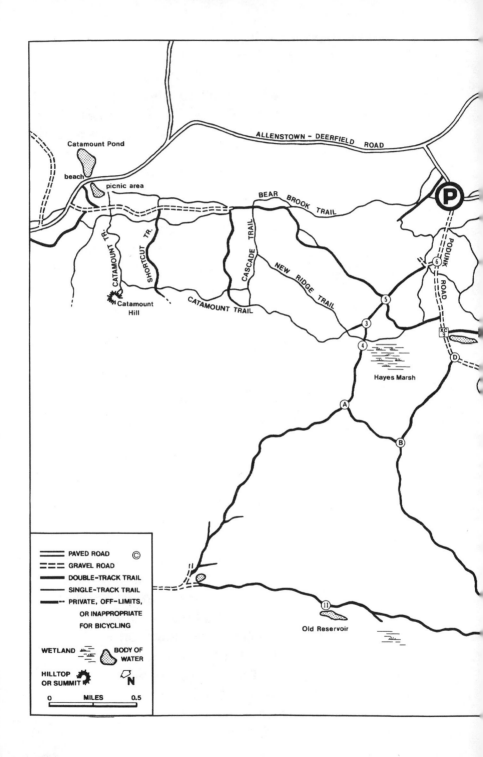

Catamount Pond

beach

picnic area

ALLENSTOWN – DEERFIELD ROAD

P

BEAR BROOK TRAIL

CATAMOUNT TR.

SHORTCUT TR.

CASCADE TRAIL

NEW RIDGE TRAIL

PODUNK ROAD

Catamount Hill

CATAMOUNT TRAIL

5

6

3

4

XC

D

Hayes Marsh

A

B

11

Old Reservoir

PAVED ROAD ©

GRAVEL ROAD

DOUBLE-TRACK TRAIL

SINGLE-TRACK TRAIL

PRIVATE, OFF-LIMITS,
OR INAPPROPRIATE
FOR BICYCLING

WETLAND

BODY OF
WATER

HILLTOP
OR SUMMIT

N

0   MILES   0.5

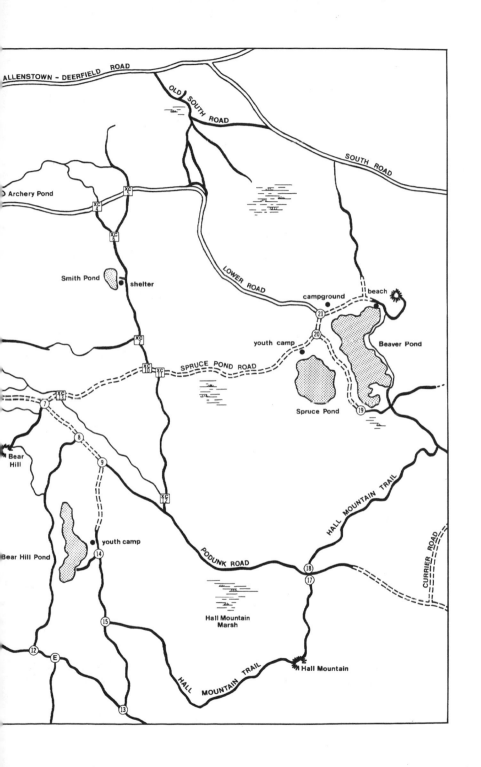

descent to the road a single-track intersects on the left and gradually climbs to the tree-covered summit of Bear Hill, where a concrete foundation is all that remains of a fire tower once marking the top. Ascending Bear Hill directly from Podunk Road is a much steeper approach.

Visiting **Old Reservoir** also requires plenty of daylight and energy. The trip provides a good look at what the early settlers called *hardscrabble*, a land littered with boulders and wrinkled with small hills. It is a constantly changing display and provides appealing scenery. The trail, and the park's sprawling acreage, continue far beyond Old Reservoir and the pedaling is enjoyable. After passing a small pond and emerging on a gravel road, turn right and ride uphill past a collection of side trails to return to **Hayes Marsh**. Beware that several intersections along this ride can be confusing.

The sparkling flow of Bear Brook passes below the parking lot on Podunk Road and proceeds to the **picnic area** and **beach** at **Catamount Pond**. Since hills dominate the surrounding terrain, nearby trails have generally intermediate or difficult riding. The challenging **Bear Brook Trail** clings to the banks of the stream for much of its course and makes a tricky bike ride. Beginning below the parking lot with an intermediate rating, the trail becomes confined to a narrow cat-walk by the increasing slope of the hillside, then descends to a streamside barrage of tight corners and quick transitions. Although thick moss and tall hemlocks make the scenery look peaceful, this single-track is a treacherous ride.

High above, the **Catamount Trail** challenges technical riders to survive its tight corners and rock-infested course. Named for the cats which once lurked in these woods, the trail tackles steep hills and demands precise maneuvering and plenty of patience. Though the mile-long climb up **Catamount Hill** from Catamount Pond will undoubtedly require some carrying, the remainder of the trail continues along the crest of a ridgeline with more moderate grades. Partial views await at certain points. Several routes link the Catamount and Bear Brook trails, with double-tracks like the **Shortcut Trail** being the easiest choices and narrow footpaths like **Cascade Trail** and **New Ridge Trail** requiring greater ability.

Driving Directions:
Coming from the south, take Exit 9N from Interstate 93 and follow Route 28 north for 11 miles to Deerfield Road, marked by a large, brown sign for Bear Brook State Park. The toll booth is 1 mile ahead on Deerfield Road, and Podunk Road is 2 miles beyond on the right, after a small cemetery.

From the north, take Exit 13 from Interstate 93 and follow Route 3 south for 6.5 miles, turn left (north) on Route 28 and find Deerfield Road 3 miles ahead.

Bike Shops:
Banagan's Cycling Company, 27 S. Main St., Concord, (603) 225-3330

Don's Family Sports Center, 1158 Hooksett Rd., Hooksett, (603) 644-5464

S&W Sport Shop, 238 S. Main St., Concord, (603) 228-1441

True Sport, 8 Loudon Rd., Concord, (603) 228-8411

USGS Maps:
Suncook Quadrangle

Additional Information:
Bear Brook State Park, RR#1, Box 507, Allenstown, NH 03275, Tel. (603) 485-9874

9
Hopkinton-Everett Reservoir
Dunbarton

The trails of the Hopkinton-Everett Reservoir have been created by motorized dirt bikes and ATVs and are an exciting ride for bicyclists. A dizzying collection of single-tracks winds through the woods with irrestible appeal while a network of abandoned roads lies waiting for easier pedaling. It is a popular place to ride and a frequent site for mountain bike races.

The Hopkinton-Everett Reservoir is a flood control area constructed by the U.S. Army Corps of Engineers. Following severe damage in the Merrimack Valley from storms in 1936 and 1938, the federal government initiated a series of five flood control projects throughout the watershed. The Hopkinton-Everett project, completed in 1962, involves a 6200-acre area and several dams which control two of the Merrimack's tributary rivers. Since this is a dry reservoir the dams are designed to hold water only when floods threaten the valley below, and the area is open to recreational use. It is managed by the U.S. Army Corps of Engineers and New Hampshire's Division of Forests and Lands.

Given the area's heavy use by off-road motorcycles and all-terrain vehicles, many of the trails have been severely eroded and the washed-out hills, exposed tree roots, and deep ruts have become a concern. State personnel warn that, since their primary responsibility is to protect the resource, it is possible that trails will be closed indefinitely if damage is not controlled. Much trail work has been done, including the reinforcement of steep hills with an underlayment of concrete blocks, the construction of bridges across streams and mudholes, and the placement of small signs to keep traffic from wandering off the trails. These efforts may or may not be enough to save the future, and all visitors are urged to tread extra lightly. Many routes scale steep hills and carve sharp corners, making them particularly vulnerable in wet conditions. Keep to the well-drained gravel roads if it has rained recently and expect a ban on riding during mud season, which typically lasts through May. Obey all trail closures and remember to read trailhead notices for current regulations.

Fortunately trail names, signs, and intersection numbers have been established to help visitors navigate through the bewildering network of single-tracks. One of the most popular is the 3.5-mile **Stark Pond Loop** which leaves from the parking lot and takes an intermediate course through the woods. Though its hills are less intimidating than those found on the other loops, the constant flow of turns and transitions requires agile pedaling. The only hindrance is a large, sandy area at the far end of the loop, where bicycle tires become mired. The trail finishes along the shoreline of **Stark Pond**, named for the Revolutionary War General John Stark who uttered New Hampshire's famous motto, *Live free or die*. He is buried in a cemetery on nearby **Mansion Road**.

The 4-mile **Sugar Hill Loop** is mostly intermediate riding but contains several difficult sections. The challenge comes from steep ascents and descents such as the pair at Horseshoe Hill, identified by a wooden sign where the trail drops off a low ridge, turns 90 degrees right, then scrambles back uphill. Bridges cross the major brooks but mudholes and wet spots slow the riding until the loop joins **Bassett Mill Road**.

Longer, more gradual ups and downs characterize the **Hanglider Hill Loop**. It begins from Bassett Mill Road with a rocky, technical climb to the top of a small hill, then descends in similar fashion on the opposite side to Intersection 7 and **Old Route 77**. Continuing across the road, the loop turns right at Intersection 8 and enjoys a brief

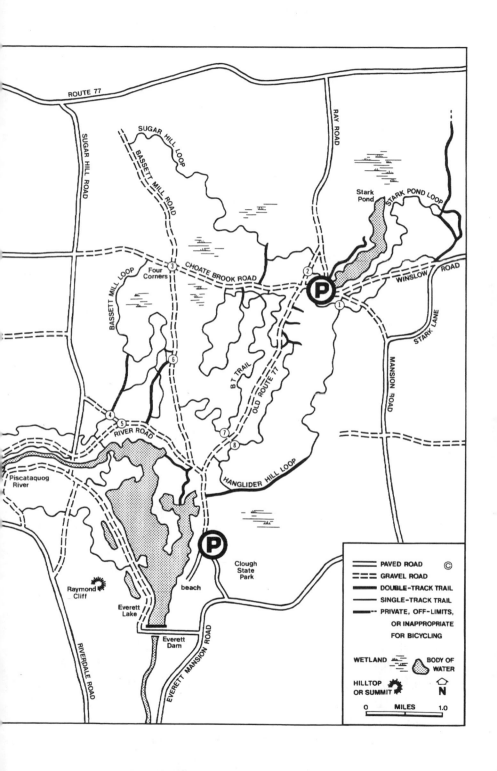

ROUTE 77

SUGAR HILL ROAD

SUGAR HILL LOOP

BASSETT MILL ROAD

RAY ROAD

Stark Pond

STARK POND LOOP

BASSETT MILL LOOP

Four Corners

3

CHOATE BROOK ROAD

WINSLOW ROAD

2

P

1

STARK LANE

6

MANSION ROAD

B T TRAIL

OLD ROUTE 77

4

5

RIVER ROAD

7

8

Piscataquog River

HANGLIDER HILL LOOP

P

Clough State Park

Raymond Cliff

beach

Everett Lake

Everett Dam

RIVERDALE ROAD

EVERETT MANSION ROAD

PAVED ROAD   ©
GRAVEL ROAD
DOUBLE-TRACK TRAIL
SINGLE-TRACK TRAIL
PRIVATE, OFF-LIMITS,
OR INAPPROPRIATE
FOR BICYCLING

WETLAND   BODY OF WATER

HILLTOP OR SUMMIT   N

0   MILES   1.0

flat section before tackling another long, uphill pedal to an open view of the horizon. It then returns abruptly to the valley floor and follows Stark Brook to Intersection 1 and **Winslow Road**, not far from the parking lot.

Difficult riding can also be found on the **BT Trail**, where a fast and furious series of hills is spiced with rocks and roots. Wrapping around the terrain in a convoluted course, it is classified as an expert trail for the motorized crowd so expect to dismount for many unrideable areas. **Bassett Mill Loop** is a similar ride of sharp turns and demanding transitions.

The gravel roads which crisscross the area offer quieter mountain biking in the flatter areas beside streams and open meadows. A contrast to the aggressive motorcycle trails, these were once the public roads of East Weare and were lined with farmhouses, schools, and cemeteries before the flood control project forced relocation to higher ground. Crumbling pavement is still evident in places. An easy, 3.7-mile loop can be made from the Stark Pond parking lot by taking **Choate Brook Road** west over a low ridge, where areas of loose rocks roughen the surface, to **Four Corners**. Turn left on Bassett Mill Road and ride to the end, turn left on **River Road**, then left again on Old Route 77 to return to the parking area.

River Road offers a nice extension to this ride. It continues for 2 miles west of Bassett Mill Road before ending on **Riverdale Road**, following the peaceful flow of the **Piscataquog River** most of the way. It is an easy and worthwhile trip through pretty scenery. When the water level is low it is possible to wade across the Piscataquog to reach the trails and roads west of **Everett Lake**, where easy gravel surfaces extend from Riverdale Road and more hilly, motorcycle routes wind through the woods. In the opposite direction River Road reaches **Clough State Park**, where a sandy **beach** awaits riders ready to plunge into the lake. Towering in the distance is the 2,000-foot-long **Everett Dam**, which stands at a height of 115 feet above the water. The

74

park and its picnic area are a popular destination on weekends.

Driving Directions:
From Interstate 89 take Exit 2 and follow Route 13 south to Pages Corner, where a flashing yellow light marks a junction with Route 77. Turn left and continue south on Route 13 for 0.7 miles, then turn right on Winslow Road. Drive for another 0.7 miles and bear right on a dirt road at the sign for OHRV Parking. This is still Winslow Road, and the Stark Pond parking area is less than a mile ahead.

For Clough State Park continue on the pavement (Stark Lane) for another 0.7 miles. At the end turn left on Mansion Road and drive for 1.3 miles, then turn right on Everett Mansion Road and the park is 1.2 miles ahead on the right. An admission fee is charged for parking at Clough during the summer.

Bike Shops:
Banagan's Cycling Company, 27 S. Main St., Concord, (603) 225-3330

Ped'ling Fool, 77 W. Main St., Hillsborough, (603) 464-5286, Rentals Available

S&W Sport Shop, 238 S. Main St., Concord, (603) 228-1441

True Sport, 8 Loudon Rd., Concord, (603) 228-8411

USGS Maps:
Hopkinton Quadrangle, Weare Quadrangle

Additional Information:
U. S. Army Corps of Engineers, New England Division, 424 Trapelo Road, Waltham, MA 02254-9149

Park Office, Hopkinton-Everett Lake, Box 210, RR2, Contoocook, NH 03229, Tel. (603) 746-4775

New Hampshire Department of Resources and Economic Development, Division of Forests and Lands, P.O. Box 856, Concord, NH 03301, Tel. (603) 271-3457

New Hampshire Department of Resources and Economic Development, Division of Parks and Recreation, Bureau of Trails, P.O. Box 856, Concord, NH 03301, Tel. (603) 271-3254

10
Fox State Forest
Hillsborough

Fox Forest is a goldmine of trails. Complete with signs displaying names and destinations, tree blazes marking every route, and a map and guide booklet describing its unique natural features, this dense trail network leaves little chance of having the same ride twice. Though plenty of challenging riding is born of the forest's hilly terrain and rough trails, easy pedaling routes can also be found.

A 1,445-acre tract with 20 miles of trails, the forest originated in 1922 from a donation by Caroline A. Fox, who offered the state her summer home, land, and a trust fund to maintain the property. The house now serves as Forest Headquarters. Located next door is the Fox Environmental Center, built in 1972 to help educate the public on the importance of the natural environment.

Fox Forest has several designated *Natural Areas*, places exhibiting features uncommon to the New Hampshire environment, and the staff asks that visitors make every effort to minimize impacts while admiring them. Stay on the trails and be careful not to disturb the fragile surroundings. Fortunately mountain bikes are welcome throughout the forest so that even bicyclists can enjoy, and respect, these interesting sights. Fox Forest is a popular place for walking, so remember to share the trails. *No Wheeled Vehicles* signs are meant to exclude motorized usage.

Many of the double-track trails exploring the area are old wagon roads once used to connect the farms and fields which dominated these hills years ago. The stone walls lining the way stretch into the woods as a reminder of these forgotten fields, now shaded by deep woods. Years of use have caused wear and the hills and rocky soils have invited erosion, so expect to find intermediate biking conditions on many routes. The single-tracks are typically the most challenging trails.

Descending steeply from the parking lot, **Valley Road** drops through Hemlock Ravine to Gerry Brook in a quarter-mile test of brakes. The trail then climbs back to **Concord End Road** on a more gradual slope hampered by a few short, steep pitches, and emerges beside the **Gerry Cemetery**. The small, family burial ground contains the graves of the Gerry family, who farmed this land in the 1800's. The foundation of their homestead is evident farther up Concord End Road on the left, where trees have taken root inside the impressive rock walls.

Old Gould Pond Road leaves across from this homesite on a rutted course down to **Bog Four Corners**. **Mud Pond Road** is in even worse condition, as washouts plague the descents of the first quarter-mile until the route levels and approaches **Mud Pond**, one of the state forest's prized Natural Areas. A developing bog, the pond is a glacial kettlehole and was formed during the Ice Age when a retreating glacier left behind a huge block of ice. Step out from the shore on the boardwalk for an up-close view of the floating layer of sphagnum moss and other rare inhabitants.

Mud Pond Road terminates at **Whitney Road**, which is maintained for car traffic on its eastern end. Turn right and continue west on the trail as it drops to a small brook and then climbs to the tall shade trees and stately stone walls of **Center Road**, just downhill from the parking lot. Livened by a mix of avoidable ruts and rocks, Whitney Road completes a 3.5-mile loop with Concord End Road, Old Gould Pond Road, and Mud Pond Road.

The **Ridge Trail** is marked by distinctive red and white tree blazes and takes a circuitous route through the entire property, beginning below the parking area at Valley Road. It is an extremely technical ride at some points, and simply unrideable at others. From Valley Road it follows

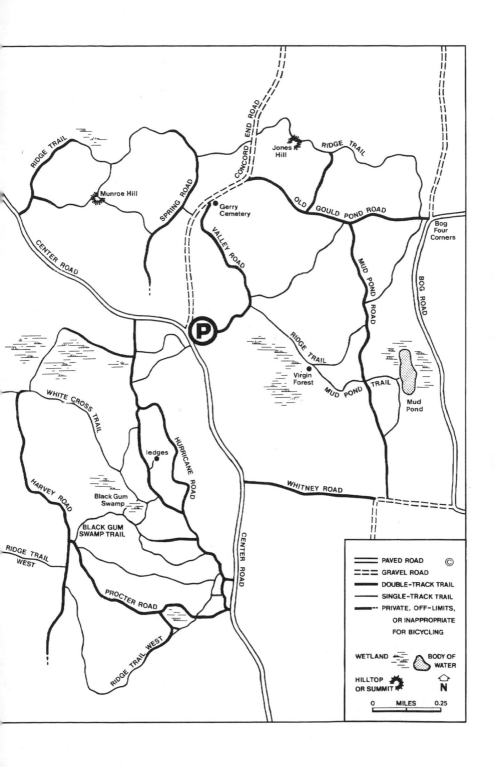

Gerry Brook to the **Virgin Forest** Natural Area, where a small tract of beech and hemlock are among the forest's oldest inhabitants. The towering trees in this area were never felled by settlers, who at one time cleared most of the surrounding land for farming. The **Mud Pond Trail** forks right at this point with a difficult ride over jumbles of rocks to Mud Pond Road, while the Ridge Trail continues left with a steep climb. It joins Mud Pond Road for about 700 feet before reentering the woods and bobbing along flatter ground to Bog Four Corners.

After crossing Old Gould Pond Road the Ridge Trail climbs the steep and rock-strewn slope of **Jones Hill**, where it is unrideable for much of the way. Either avoid this segment of the trail or plan on hiking large portions of it. The highest point at Fox Forest, neighboring **Munroe Hill** is more hospitable to bicycling but still requires difficult ascents and descents. The Ridge Trail follows **Spring Road** for a short distance, then circles Munroe Hill before climbing to the top, where a small tower awaits with a southern view of both Crotched Mountain and Mount Monadnock.

Across Center Road is a dense network of trails, posing a confusing array of intersections but plenty of riding. The **Ridge Trail West** leaves directly across from the parking lot on a path descending through a deep, dark evergreen forest to **Hurricane Road**, a fairly easy pedal throughout its entire length. As the Ridge Trail West continues along the outskirts of the state forest it ventures to some of its most remote places. Lack of use makes it difficult to follow in places. The trail crosses **Harvey Road** and **Procter Road**, two easy woods roads, follows Hurricane Road for a short distance, then bears left to climb a low ridge, where the **ledges** provide a partial view to the east, best after the leaves have fallen.

The **Black Gum Swamp Trail** passes through the middle of **Black Gum Swamp**, another of the forest's designated Natural Areas, and is unfit for bicycling.

Take a short excursion up Center Road to

Hillsborough Center. Only a few minutes up the hill, the picturesque village appears unchanged from its early days, and circling the common will bring a step back in time. It is a classic New England village of white clapboards and granite posts, far removed from the hustle of modern day life.

Driving Directions:
From Interstate 89 take Exit 5 for Routes 9 and 202 West. Continue to the traffic signal in Hillsborough at the intersection of Route 149, and turn right on School Street, following signs to Hillsborough Center. School Street eventually becomes Center Road, and the Fox State Forest parking lot is 2 miles ahead on the right.

Bike Shops:
The Ped'ling Fool, 77 W. Main St., Hillsborough, (603) 464-5286, Rentals Available

USGS Maps:
Hillsborough Quadrangle

Additional Information:
Fox State Forest, P. O. Box 1175, Hillsborough, NH 03244, Tel. (603) 464-3453

11
Pillsbury State Park
Washington

Spared the attention and development of other parks, Pillsbury remains a quiet place of solitary ponds and unspoiled woodlands. The park's little-known 5,250 acres are an unexpected find in the shadow of Mount Sunapee, and are home to miles of footpaths and old logging roads. Much of the mountain biking is challenging and will test even the most experienced riders.

Originally known as Cherry Valley for its abundance of the trees, this property was owned by Albert Pillsbury until he deeded it to the public in 1920. Mr. Pillsbury was a founder of the Society for the Preservation of New Hampshire Forests, an organization dedicated to preserving woodlands and protecting the state's natural scenery. Today Pillsbury State Park is a welcome retreat for camping, fishing, hiking, and off-road cycling. Staff is present only during the summer months, when a fee is charged. But be mindful that many of the trails are not dry until June since some areas are poorly drained and high in elevation. The park is also a trailhead for hikers so expect to meet others on the trail.

The gravel road accessing Pillsbury State Park from **Route 31** follows the northern shore of **May Pond**, where secluded campsites sit at the water's edge. There is room to park at the end of the road at a meadow and picnic area overlooking **Mill Pond**. Once the site of a sawmill, this open area is the starting point to several logging roads which branch into the woods. A footbridge spans the stream near the mill's stone foundation and delivers bicyclists to one of Pillsbury's nicest pedaling trails, the misnamed **Mad Road**. It is a pleasant, 3.5-mile ride under the shade of birch and beech trees, with grass growing in the center of the old road. Bicyclists cruise easily past **Bacon Pond**, but halfway along must struggle up a half-mile climb and then descend on a bumpy slope. The trail levels as it traverses a hillside above **Fletcher Pond** and emerges on Route 31. Returning on the pavement is a mostly downhill ride and completes a 6.5-mile loop.

The more challenging **Five Summers Trail**, named for the period of time required for its construction during the 1950's, leaves from the opposite side of the parking lot and climbs gradually on the course of an old logging road. After passing a spur to scenic **North Pond**, where the **Clemac Trail** departs on an unrideable course up **Bryant Mountain**, the trail becomes rougher with rocks and ruts and begins a long ascent. Although the majority of hills are eroded, occasional downhills provide rest and snowmobile bridges span the streams encountered. The trail eventually narrows, forks with a snowmobile route, then climbs through a beech forest, dodging rock ledges and scaling pitches much too steep for bicycling before reaching the top, 4 miles from the parking lot.

The Five Summers Trail ends on the **Monadnock-Sunapee Greenway**, a 49-mile hiking trail linking Mounts Monadnock and Sunapee over a combination of private and public lands. The Greenway is managed by the Society for the Preservation of New Hampshire Forests and maintained by the New Hampshire Chapter of the Appalachian Mountain Club, and both groups ask that users show proper respect for the unique trail. Although privately-owned portions are off-limits for bicycling, the distance within Pillsbury is open for expert riders. Short carries are required at many points where the trail traverses slopes too steep to ride, but if you do not mind the extra work the Greenway is an enjoyable trip. White tree blazes mark the way.

Following the Greenway north from the Five Summers Trail involves significant amounts of hiking, especially near **Lucia's Lookout**. Although tree-covered,

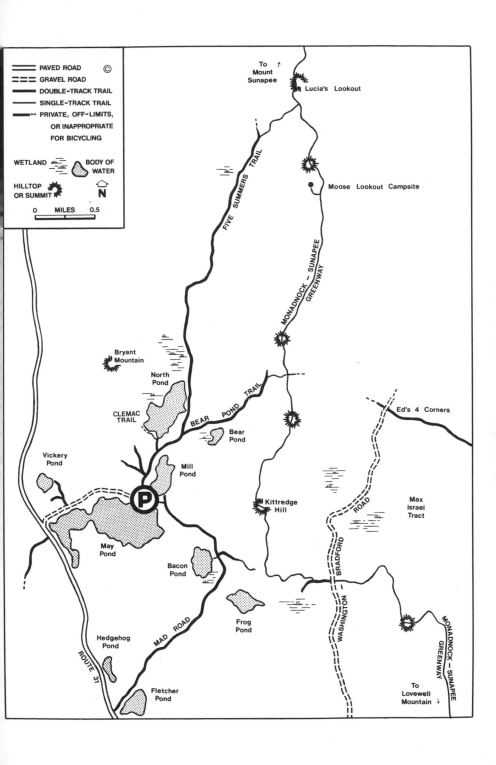

this rocky knoll gives nice views in all directions from its various corners. The trail extends northward for another 4.2 miles through a narrow strip of land known as the Pillsbury-Sunapee Corridor, then ends at the 2743-foot summit of **Mount Sunapee**. Spectacular views of Sunapee Lake and the White Mountains make it an appealing destination, but extensive carrying is required.

Heading south on the Greenway is a more rideable option since the terrain is milder. The trail follows the crest of a ridge which divides the Connecticut and Merrimack river valleys, with many sections being a surprisingly smooth and easy ride in the shade of hardwood forest. A short spur leads to **Moose Lookout Campsite**, merely a clearing in the woods. After 3 miles the **Bear Pond Trail**, blazed in blue, appears at a clearly marked intersection and descends for 1.3 miles back to Five Summers Trail, dropping gently for the first half-mile then more steeply after joining an old logging road. The trail's direct line down the slope has invited erosion and bicyclists must choose careful lines to avoid the washouts. Flatter ground reappears near **Bear Pond** but wet spots make the pedaling difficult. Combining Five Summers Trail, Monadnock-Sunapee Greenway, and Bear Pond Trail makes an 8-mile loop from the parking area, and is best ridden in the clockwise direction since the ascents are more gradual.

Continuing southward, the Greenway encounters more steep terrain at the slopes of **Kittredge Hill**, where hiking is required. The trail maneuvers through tight quarters with rocks and trees forming a challenging course. After descending to Bog Brook and **Washington-Bradford Road** it again tackles impossible uphill grades as it rises to **Lovewell Mountain** in the south. Once the primary means of travelling between the two towns, Washington-Bradford Road passes stone walls and ancient sugar maple trees, and makes a refreshingly easy mountain bike ride. It accesses the **Max Israel Tract**, a state-owned property adjacent to Pillsbury. Much of the road has been improved for logging operations, and it is an easy ride southward to the picture-perfect village of Washington, the first town to incorporate in 1776 under the leadership of George Washington.

Driving Directions:
Coming from the south, take Exit 5 from Interstate 89 and follow Route 9 west through Hillsborough to Route 31. Turn right and drive north on Route 31, and look for the park's entrance 4 miles north of the center of Washington.

From the north find Route 31 less than a mile past the center of Goshen, forking left. The park is 5 miles south on the left side. Park at the end of the gravel road, being careful not to block access to the trailhead.

Bike Shops:
Bob Skinner's Ski & Sports, Route 103, Mt. Sunapee Traffic Circle, Mount Sunapee, (603) 763-2303, Rentals Available

Lane Road Cycle Shop, Lover's Lane Road, Charlestown, (603) 826-4435

Ped'ling Fool, 77 W. Main St., Hillsborough, (603) 464-5286, Rentals Available

USGS Map:
Sunapee Quadrangle, Lovewell Mountain Quadrangle

Additional Information:
New Hampshire Department of Resources and Economic Development, Division of Parks and Recreation, P. O. Box 856, Concord, NH 03301-0856, Tel. (603) 271-3254

Society for the Preservation of New Hampshire Forests, 54 Portsmouth Street, Concord, NH 03301, Tel. (603) 224-9945

12
Back Roads
Strafford and Farmington

Mountain biking is a great way to explore New Hampshire's quiet countryside, and the unsurfaced roads of Strafford and Farmington offer ideal opportunities. These dirt roads are a welcome relief from the pavement of nearby towns as they explore a rolling patchwork of farmland and forest. In addition to the obstacle-free cruising on gravel roads, there is plenty of challenging riding on Class VI roads which thread through the hills with forgotten appeal.

Contrary to the maintained routes, the Class VI roads in Strafford are not always marked and can be difficult to identify since they appear only as trails. Some are disguised as driveways, others are obscured by brush. Those in Farmington are more apparent because large, white signs mark their endpoints with the message, *Road not Maintained, Subject to Gates and Bars*. Half-forgotten, these old roads are still public property and remain open for enjoyment, but always remember that the land and trails beside them are private.

Blue Job Mountain is the area's focal point. A state forest surrounds the small mountain and several trails lead from the parking lot to the top, but all are posted as being off-limits to bicycling. Take a few minutes on foot to visit the summit's lookout tower and great view, which includes both the Atlantic Ocean and the White Mountains. The trailhead is only 400 feet in elevation below the top. It is a popular hike on clear days so parking at the trailhead could be limited.

Several old roads surround Blue Job with a 4.2-mile loop of intermediate riding. Begin about 100 feet uphill of the parking area on **First Crown Point Road** where a rough double-track rises gradually into the woods between two private homes. This old road crosses the state forest boundary several times as it skirts the mountain's southern slope and descends toward **Oxbow Pond**. After a mile turn left on a rutted double-track and continue for 1.5 miles to **Scruton Road**, another Class VI road. Turn left and First Crown Point Road is a mile away.

First Crown Point Road originated in the late 1700's when settlers ventured inland from the coast. Laid out in a northwesterly direction, the road facilitated trade and communication with seaports like Portsmouth. Its history is revealed by the old houses and tall shade trees along the way, and much of the surrounding land continues to be farmed. From **Strafford Corner**, First Crown Point Road rises gently through pastures and corn fields for almost 2 miles, then begins a more serious, mile-long climb to the trailhead parking area below Blue Job. This last mile gains 400 feet in elevation, an important detail to remember when finishing a long ride. The parking area is at the crest of a long ridgeline of low hills which extends southwestward to **Mack Mountain** and **Parker Mountain**. Much of the hill climbing in the Strafford and Farmington area involves traversing this elevation.

A half-mile away **Second Crown Point Road** parallels this course, advancing through farmland to forest on surfaces of pavement, gravel, and then trail. Beginning at **Route 202**, the road changes to gravel after 2 miles and degrades to trail after another 1.5 miles. It then begins to climb through **Barn Door Gap**, a narrow pass below **Sanders Ledge**. The climb is badly eroded in places and ends after another mile at the smooth gravel of **Barn Door Gap Road**, which descends on an enjoyable, 3-mile coast to **Wingate Road** near the North Barnstead town line.

Look for **Little Niagara Road** on the right, halfway down Barn Door Gap Road. A Class VI road, it holds some of the area's finest scenery and carries an intermediate rating. After a steep but brief descent the old road passes

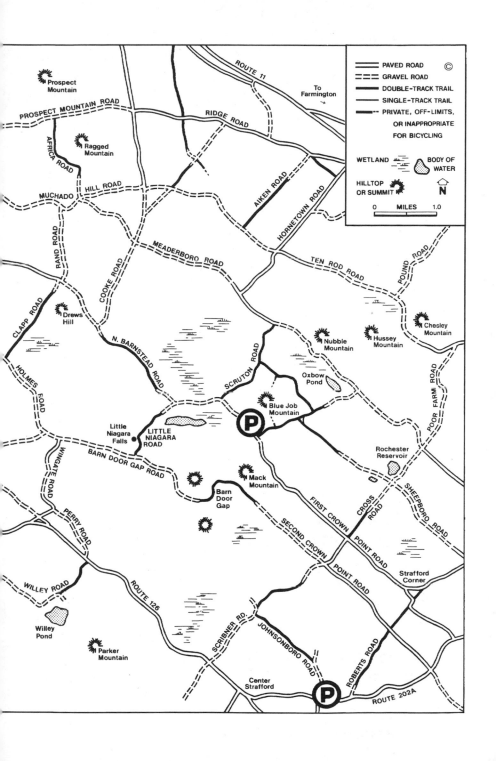

Little Niagara Falls, a small waterfall flowing over an open ledge, then continues around a beaver pond, rises up a hill to a small cemetery, and descends past an open wetland to the end of First Crown Point Road. Its total length is 1.3 miles. Together with First Crown Point Road, **Cross Road**, and Second Crown Point Road it forms a 9.5-mile loop from the Blue Job parking area.

Cross Road links many other roads to create good mountain biking loops. South of Second Crown Point Road it drops down rocky slopes to a brook, then rises to the end of **Scribner Road**. Here **Johnsonboro Road** runs easterly for a mile to Route 202A, emerging at a turnout and parking area. Several low points create large puddles and it is an intermediate ride. Challenging **Roberts Road** begins nearby, traversing two small hills before flattening with a smooth, grassy surface near Second Crown Point Road. Combining Cross Road with Johnsonboro Road, Roberts Road, and Second Crown Point Road creates a difficult, 6.5-mile ride.

The northern end of Cross Road passes **Rochester Reservoir** and then intersects **Meaderboro Road** and **Poor Farm Road**, two quiet, country roads. Meaderboro begins at Route 202A with a familiar northwesterly course, rolling with the hills and enjoying several views of Blue Job Mountain. It climbs for most of its final 1.2 miles beyond **Cooke Road** in an area of open farmland. For a 12-mile loop, ride First Crown Point Road downhill for 2 miles, turn left on Cooke Road, then left on Meaderboro and continue for 6 miles to a four-way intersection. Turn left on Cooke Road and ride to the end, then turn left on **North Barnstead Road** which degrades to an intermediate trail before returning to the end of First Crown Point Road.

Ten Rod Road offers a good extension to this ride, and can be combined with Poor Farm Road for an obstacle-free cruise. Stop off at the area's old dog pound, easily distinguished by its massive, 10-foot walls of stone. It is a short distance up unmarked **Pound Road**, which leaves Ten

Rod Road opposite a wetland below **Hussey** and **Chesley Mountains**. Built in 1822, the relic will likely be standing for many years to come. Pound Road continues up a small hill before dropping on a rutted course to **Route 11** near the center of **Farmington**.

Driving Directions:
From the Spaulding Turnpike take Exit 14. At the end of the ramp turn right on Ten Rod Road, then turn right (south) on Route 11. After a half-mile turn hard right on Route 202A and continue west for 2.7 miles to Crown Point Road, which joins First Crown Point Road after another 2 miles. Blue Job trailhead parking is 5 miles from Route 202A, just beyond the end of the pavement.

Additional parking is available at a turnout on Route 202A opposite Sloper Road, 2.3 miles south of First Crown Point Road and 1.2 miles north of Center Strafford.

Bike Shops:
Durham Bike, Pettee Brook Lane, Durham, (603) 868-5634

Nordic Skier, 47 N. Main St., Wolfeboro, (603) 569-3151, Rentals Available

Philbrick's Sport Center, 161 Portland Ave. (Rte. 4), Dover, (603) 742-9333

Piche's Ski & Sport Shop, Lehner St., Wolfeboro, (603) 569-8234, Rentals Available

USGS Maps:
Alton Quadrangle

13
Gunstock Recreation Area
Gilford

High above New Hampshire's grandest lake, Winnipesaukee, Gunstock is a treasure of trails in the midst of one of New England's most popular summer attractions. The year-round recreation area is owned by Belknap County and includes a popular campground, ski jumps, hiking trails, and well-known cross country and downhill skiing facilities. Bustling with skiers in winter, the area welcomes bicyclists in summer and has designated several trails for mountain biking, a sport drawing many of the same enthusiasts. Steep terrain on many trails is balanced by stunning views of both the White Mountains and Lakes Region, and adds a rewarding flavor to much of the riding.

Visitors to Gunstock are requested to stay out of the **campground** area and avoid all trails west of the access road during the camping season. The staff also asks that bicyclists respect the problem of erosion by not riding when conditions are wet, especially on the poorly drained cross country trails. Although these wide, grassy trails may look welcoming, some are plagued by wet spots and will need extra time to dry out after rainy periods. Other routes scale the area's steep hills and will deteriorate rapidly if ridden when wet. Understand the concerns of those who maintain these trails and use careful judgement when riding the routes that are at risk.

Gunstock's designated mountain biking routes are each clearly labeled with signs. The **Cobble Mountain Trail** is the easiest, and it forms the backbone to the cross country ski trail network with a trouble-free, 2-mile cruise around **Cobble Mountain**. Cutting a broad swath designed to provide plenty of space for gliding skiers, the gravelly trail is well-drained and offers a silky smooth surface for pedaling, but requires a significant hill climb when taking the loop from either direction.

Several short side trips can liven up the Cobble Mountain Trail for riders with extra energy, but be sure that the ground is firm and dry before starting. The **Knoll Loop** scrambles abruptly up a short hill only to turn and immediately drop back to the main trail. Similarly, both the **Wood Loop** and **Race Loop** provide short but steep diversions.

Other trails lead to more remote destinations. Pack a lunch and try the grassy **Rock Loop** which makes a half-mile-long excursion to a picnic table overlooking a wetland along Poorfarm Brook. For a longer ride combine the **Birch Trail** and **Maple Trail** to form a 2-mile circuit, with a cut-off at the halfway point. Though these trails are only suitable for bicycling under dry conditions, they are smoothed by a forgiving, grassy surface. Labeled as difficult for skiers, the Maple Trail is only intermediate for bicyclists, with hill climbs being the primary challenge. The two trails join in a small meadow where another picnic table provides a good lunching spot. Old stone walls and occasional barbed wire stretch through the woods near these trails as reminders of past farm fields.

A confusing array of options fan out in front of the campground office, where Cobble Mountain rises steadily to the east. Look for the uphill switchbacks of **Recurve** to lead up this thigh-bursting bump where two outlooks give beautiful views. Follow **Compound** for a look toward the downhill ski area and **Target** for a bird's eye view over Lake Winnipesaukee. Cobble Mountain is aptly named because at several points high on this 1400-foot hill it appears to be a huge pile of rocks, requiring bicyclists to pedal carefully.

If Cobble Mountain is not punishment enough, rest assured that the gear-grinding climb up **Gunstock Mountain** will be. With base elevation at 1000 feet and the summit at nearly 2300 feet, the **Flintlock Trail** puts the

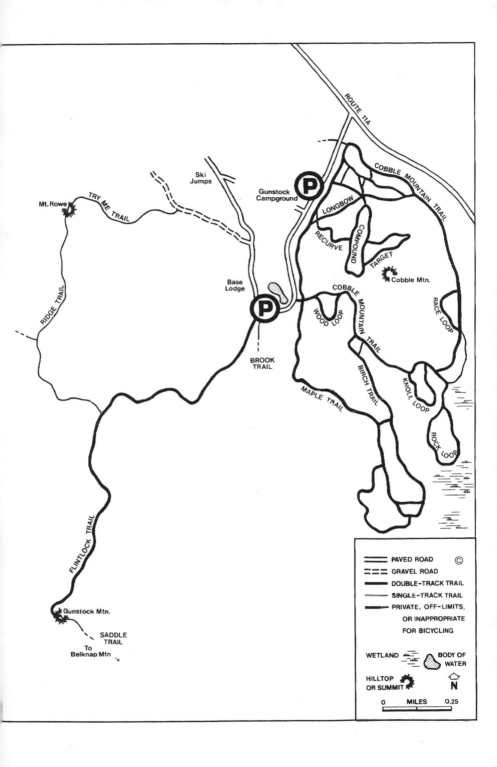

ROUTE 11A

Ski
Jumps

Gunstock
Campground

COBBLE MOUNTAIN TRAIL

Mt. Rowe

TRY ME TRAIL

LONGBOW

RECURVE

COMPOUND

TARGET

Cobble Mtn.

RIDGE TRAIL

Base
Lodge

COBBLE MOUNTAIN TRAIL

WOOD LOOP

RACE LOOP

BROOK
TRAIL

MAPLE TRAIL

BIRCH TRAIL

KNOLL LOOP

ROCK LOOP

FLINTLOCK TRAIL

Gunstock Mtn.

SADDLE
TRAIL
To
Belknap Mtn

PAVED ROAD   ©
GRAVEL ROAD
DOUBLE-TRACK TRAIL
SINGLE-TRACK TRAIL
PRIVATE, OFF-LIMITS,
OR INAPPROPRIATE
FOR BICYCLING

WETLAND   BODY OF
                 WATER

HILLTOP   N
OR SUMMIT

0   MILES   0.25

mountain into mountain biking, asking bicyclists to scale 1300 feet in just 1.7 miles. Few thighs will be strong enough to pedal all the way to the top, but the summit views are a worthy reward even if you have to walk your bike all or part of the way. The panorama over Lake Winnipesaukee with Mount Washington on the horizon is a spectacular sight. Meant only for experienced riders, the Flintlock Trail is a service road and begins near the **base lodge** at the main parking lot, to the left of the Summit Triple Chair and to the right of a large, stone fireplace. The climb alternates between steep pitches and more gradual traverses, a combination too strenuous for most riders. The gravelly surface is loose and hampered by rough rocks in places, and the downhill return is a long, steep test of brakes, so be sure to check them before starting.

Gunstock Mountain was named in pioneer times when a local hunter encountered a wildcat on the slope. As the tale goes, the startled hunter was only a few feet away from the cat when his trigger jammed, so in desperation he swung his rifle, killing the animal but breaking the stock of the gun in the process. Although the man's name has been forgotten his gun is immortalized on the mountain.

The **Brook Trail** also directly connects the base parking lot to the summit but is best left for hiking because big rocks and steep grades make it unrideable. Closer to the top the blue-blazed **Saddle Trail** branches southward along the ridge and it too is unrideable. Monstrous roots, treacherous rocks, and impossible grades block the way but many choose to hike the 1.3 miles of trail to the lookout tower on neighboring **Belknap Mountain** and enjoy a 360-degree view stretching from the Atlantic Ocean to the Green Mountains on a clear day. Belknap's 2384-foot summit has served as a signal and surveying station since the 1800's and can also be reached by the Belknap Carriage Road, which climbs from the town of Gilford through a state reservation on the southwestern side.

The **Ridge Trail** leaves the Flintlock near the top of

the Tiger Triple Chairlift and runs northerly along an open ridge for 0.7 miles to **Mount Rowe**, where another view of Lake Winnipesaukee awaits. The trail is exposed for much of the way, bordered by blueberry bushes and junipers as it crosses broad slabs of ledge. A few technical challenges spice the trip but it is generally an intermediate ride, and although the trail dips into a saddle between the two mountains the elevation gain is relatively minor. Gunstock has been a ski area since the 1940's and the remains of one of its first lifts is evident at the top of Mount Rowe. The nearby **Try Me Trail** follows the steep, winding course of a former ski trail for a mile down the mountain to the bottom.

Driving Directions:
From Interstate 93 take Exit 20 and follow Routes 3 North and 11 East for 9.5 miles. Turn right (east) on Route 11A and continue for 5.5 miles, past Gilford Village, to Gunstock's access road on the right, marked by a large sign. Find the ski area parking lot at the end of the road, or park beside the road near the campground office.

Bike Shops:
Boot 'n Wheel Cycling & Fitness, 368 Union Ave., Laconia, (603) 524-7665

Nordic Skier, 47 N. Main St., Wolfeboro, (603) 569-3151, Rentals Available

Paquette's Sporting Goods, 25 Canal St., Laconia, (603) 524-1017

Piche's Ski & Sport, 318 Gilford Ave., Laconia, (603) 524-2068, Rentals Available

Piche's Ski & Sport, Lehner St., Wolfeboro, (603) 569-8234, Rentals Available

USGS Maps:
Winnipesaukee Quadrangle

Additional Information:
Gunstock Recreation Area, Box 1307, Laconia, NH 03247, Tel. (603) 293-4341

14
Gile State Forest
Springfield

Few would expect to find so many miles of great trails and old roads off this lonely stretch of Route 4A, but those who stop to explore will not be disappointed. Gile is an ideal place for mountain biking and offers all levels of riding, from long, challenging loops to easy, gravel roads. The riding extends across an area of little-known hills where trails often reveal more moose prints than fat-tire tracks. Equidistant from Concord and Hanover, the state forest is located at the height of land between the Connecticut and Merrimack river valleys.

Many of the trails benefit from the efforts of local snowmobilers who have marked intersections with signs, built bridges, and kept the routes maintained. Bicyclists should note, however, that some snowmobile routes pass over private lands under winter-only agreements and are not necessarily open to public use in summer. Watch for the blue-blazed, state forest boundaries when riding these trails. Also note that Gile is a popular place for hunting once deer season begins, so it is not the place to ride during the late fall.

Park at the **Gardner Memorial Wayside Park**, a picnic area named for a past Springfield resident who once owned most of the state forest's acreage as part of a lumber business. It is the trailhead for only the **Butterfield Pond Trail**, a difficult path which leads across the footbridge over Kimpton Brook to **Butterfield Pond**. The trail starts on an old wagon road and then turns right on a narrower course where an abundance of stumps and rocks protrude from the ground. Bicyclists have a formidable challenge from these obstacles in the confined space of the footpath. The pond's shoreline is less than a mile away.

Several trails leave **Route 4A** a half-mile above the wayside. **Gardner Road** and **Noyes Road** are both marked by signs, and join the **King's Highway**, a double-track trail that was an important road for early settlers. It was built in 1773 to a width of one rod, a distance of about sixteen feet, but forest growth has now narrowed it considerably and the cellarholes and stonewalls along its course have become obscure. The trail is a marked snowmobile route and signs are posted at most of the intersections. Wet spots, tire ruts, and a long hill climb over the northern shoulder of **Sanborn Hill** slow the ride before it ends at a four-way intersection. One trail heads south to **Morgan Pond** on a long and rocky ride while the other options cross private lands.

Most of the mountain biking lies on the northern side of Route 4A, where long tours can be made on the area's old roads. A half-mile up **Old Grafton Road** look for a sign on the right identifying a Class VI road, open to public use but no longer maintained for regular travel. The forgotten road is great for mountain biking and encounters few obstacles as it climbs over a low ridgeline to **Kinsman Highway** in the neighboring town of Grafton. Numerous water breaks cut across the long hills have prevented erosion and the wooden bridges spanning the streams remain in good repair. The road passes the familiar blue tree blazes of the state forest boundary several times, where sharp eyes will also see old metal signs stating, *Property of Dartmouth College*. Dartmouth had acquired the land before it became a state forest. After a 1.5-mile uphill grind the road finally crests at a small cabin, loses its gravelly surface for a carpeting of grass, and begins a 2-mile descent. Dropping steeply for the first half-mile, the trail falls more gradually toward the end where there is a pretty view northward to Mount Cardigan.

Turn right on the wide, gravel surface of Kinsman Highway and ride downhill for 1.2 miles to **Robinson Corner**, merely a turn in the road. Kinsman Highway

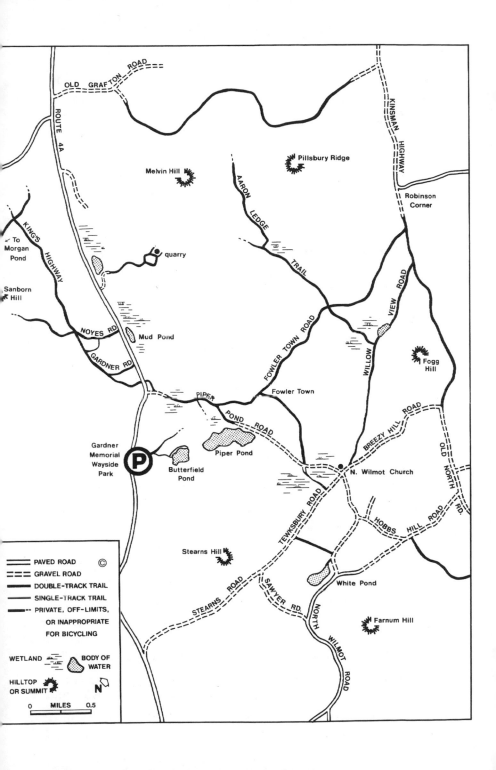

OLD GRAFTON ROAD

ROUTE 4A

KINSMAN HIGHWAY

Pillsbury Ridge

Melvin Hill

AARON LEDGE TRAIL

Robinson
Corner

KING'S HIGHWAY

To
Morgan
Pond

quarry

Sanborn
Hill

NOYES RD

GARDNER RD.

Mud Pond

FOWLER TOWN ROAD

WILLOW VIEW ROAD

Fogg
Hill

PIPER

POND ROAD

Fowler Town

BREEZY HILL ROAD

OLD NORTH RD.

Gardner
Memorial
Wayside
Park

P

Butterfield
Pond

Piper Pond

N. Wilmot Church

TEWKSBURY ROAD

HOBBS HILL ROAD

Stearns Hill

White Pond

STEARNS ROAD

SAWYER RD.

NORTH WILMOT ROAD

Farnum Hill

PAVED ROAD   ©
GRAVEL ROAD
DOUBLE-TRACK TRAIL
SINGLE-TRACK TRAIL
PRIVATE, OFF-LIMITS,
    OR INAPPROPRIATE
    FOR BICYCLING

WETLAND   BODY OF
                                    WATER

HILLTOP
OR SUMMIT   N

0   MILES   0.5

continues straight and rises as an unmaintained road up a steady slope, where two old roads branch to the right. Bicyclists should avoid **Willow View Road**, which is flooded by a large beaver pond and impassable, but can take **Fowler Town Road** for a challenging ride. It takes a hilly course along the state forest's eastern perimeter for almost 3 miles, with some sections badly eroded with exposed rocks and ledge. After a half-mile climb from Kinsman Highway the road descends for a half-mile to a four-way intersection with the **Aaron Ledge Trail**, a marked snowmobile route. Aaron Ledge Trail takes an uphill course with both single- and double-track riding to **Pillsbury Ridge**, but eventually leaves the state forest for private property.

Continuing on Fowler Town Road becomes easier as the road has been upgraded for logging operations. Look for **Fowler Town** at the next intersection, 1.2 miles ahead, where a small settlement flourished in the mid-1800's. The cellarholes of several homes and a schoolhouse are now concealed by the woods but a tiny cemetery is visible beside the road. It serves as a reminder that this route has been in use for more than 150 years. The improved road turns sharply left as Fowler Town Road continues straight, descending for a half-mile in step-like pitches to the ruts of **Piper Pond Road**. Turn right to return to Route 4A. Combining Route 4A, Old Grafton Road, Kinsman Highway, Fowler Town Road, and Piper Pond Road forms an ambitious, 13.5-mile loop from the wayside.

Piper Pond Road is driveable by car between **Piper Pond** and the immaculate, white clapboard **North Wilmot Church**. Built in 1829, the church stands alone in the woods but is the focal point to an area of dirt roads and small farms known as North Wilmot. For an easy, 4-mile loop from the church try **Breezy Hill Road**, **Old North Road**, and **Hobbs Hill Road**. Car traffic is sparse on these gently rolling country roads and they provide all the stillness and solitude of a trail. **Tewksbury Road** is in slightly rougher condition as it rises and falls over bigger hills. It stretches for 1.3 miles to **Stearns Road**, which descends for another 1.5 miles to Route 4A. Combining Piper Pond Road, Tewksbury Road, Stearns Road, and Route 4A makes an easy, 8-mile circuit from the wayside.

Driving Directions:

From Interstate 89 take Exit 11 and drive east on Route 11 for 7 miles to Route 4A, just before a Mobil station. Turn left (north) on Route 4A and continue for 7 miles to the Gardner Memorial Wayside Park, on the right.

Bike Shops:

Bob Skinner's Ski & Sports, Route 103, Mt. Sunapee Traffic Circle, Mount Sunapee, (603) 763-2303, Rentals Available

New England Bicycling Center, Ragged Mountain Hwy. (Route 104), Danbury, (603) 768-3318

Omer & Bob's Sport Shop, 7 Allen St., Hanover, (603) 643-3525

Tom Mowatt Cycles, Olde Nuggett Alley, Hanover, (603) 643-5522

Tom Mowatt Cycles, 213 Mechanic St., Lebanon, (603) 448-5556

USGS Maps:

Mascoma Quadrangle, Cardigan Quadrangle, Sunapee Quadrangle, Mount Kearsarge Quadrangle

Additional Information:

New Hampshire Department of Resources and Economic Development, Division of Forests and Lands, P. O. Box 856, Concord, NH 03301-0856, Tel. (603) 271-3457

15
Back Roads
Hanover, Lyme, and Canaan

Dartmouth College students have long been drawn to the outdoors, and mountain biking has naturally become a popular activity. Although the trails close to town are either off-limits or too confined for bicycling, a wealth of options spreads through the hills to provide Hanover's energetic population with miles of great fat-tire routes. They range from unsurfaced country roads to forgotten wagon tracks and offer both short, afternoon escapes and distant, daylong tours.

Some important trail policies in the area should be noted. In addition to being restricted from the trails at Pine Park, bicycles are absolutely prohibited on the **Appalachian Trail**, which was designed, built, and protected for foot travel. Marked by white blazes, the *AT* passes through Hanover and Lyme in a protected corridor of land with boundaries blazed in yellow, and crosses several of the mountain biking routes described below. Be alert for it since not all intersections are posted with signs.

The Class VI roads shown on the accompanying map may be disguised as private driveways or obscured by brush, but they remain public property and are open to recreational use. Many side trails branch from these mountain biking routes onto private property though, so get the landowner's permission before riding them.

The lack of a trailhead in the area leaves few parking options for those ariving by car, but ample space exists at the **Dartmouth Skiway** in Lyme. Adequate roadside parking can also be found at several points along the surrounding road system, especially near the Appalachian Trail crossings. Wherever you choose to park, be sensitive to the needs and concerns of local residents.

Beginning at the Skiway, ride uphill on **Canaan Turnpike** which divides the ski slopes of **Winslow Ledge** from those of **Holts Ledge**. The turnpike, merely a dirt road, climbs for a mile to a low pass between these two hills and then descends for 2 miles in a series of gentle grades. Buried in deep forest, the road rises for 1.5 miles as it crosses the Canaan town line and becomes **Turnpike Road**, then gains pavement before descending to **Canaan Center**. To complete a 16-mile loop from the Skiway, turn right after 4.5 miles on **Beech Cobble Road**, then right after 1 mile on **Gould Road** and coast down the steep hillside to the shoreline of **Goose Pond**. Turn right and ride **Goose Pond Road** for 6 miles to a four-way intersection, turn right on **Hill Road** and continue for 3 miles to the end at **Lyme Center**. The Skiway is to the right, 1.2 miles uphill.

The popular, 11-mile round-trip ride from the Skiway to **Cummins Pond** is ideal for a summer afternoon and does not require advanced riding skills. Just below the Skiway turn north on **Dorchester Road**, a well-maintained gravel road leading uphill. It gradually narrows as it climbs past several houses and the **Lambert Ridge Trail** (Appalachian Trail), which ascends 3240' Smarts Mountain to the north. The road flattens by a small bog at the 3-mile mark and reaches **Reservoir Pond** after another half-mile. It then follows the southern shore to the Lyme-Dorchester town line, where a sign warns travelers that the road is no longer maintained. Here it is called **Cummins Pond Road** and degrades to a four wheel drive route with large puddles measuring the full width of the road. Cummins Pond appears at the top of an eroded hill climb 2 miles past Reservoir Pond, and offers a rewarding view of Smarts Mountain, capped by a lookout tower. Public access to the water exists farther up the road. For the strongest riders, Cummins Pond Road continues eastward with rougher conditions for 4 more miles to the tiny village of Dorchester.

Closer to town, **Three Mile Road** is everything a

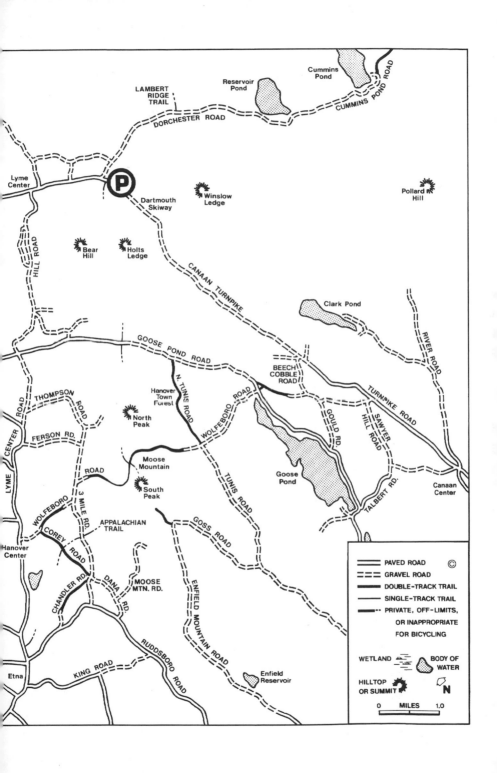

CUMMINS POND ROAD

Cummins
Pond

Reservoir
Pond

LAMBERT
RIDGE
TRAIL

DORCHESTER ROAD

CUMMINS POND ROAD

Lyme
Center

P

Dartmouth
Skiway

Winslow
Ledge

Pollard
Hill

HILL ROAD

Bear
Hill

Holts
Ledge

CANAAN TURNPIKE

Clark Pond

RIVER ROAD

GOOSE POND ROAD

BEECH
COBBLE
ROAD

TURNPIKE ROAD

THOMPSON ROAD

Hanover
Town
Forest

N. TUNIS ROAD

WOLFEBORO ROAD

GOULD RD.

SAWYER HILL ROAD

CENTER ROAD

LYME

FERSON RD.

North
Peak

ROAD

Moose
Mountain

South
Peak

TUNIS ROAD

Goose
Pond

TALBERT RD.

Canaan
Center

WOLFEBORO

3 MILE RD.

COREY ROAD

APPALACHIAN
TRAIL

GOSS ROAD

Hanover
Center

CHANDLER RD.

DANA RD.

MOOSE
MTN. RD.

ENFIELD MOUNTAIN ROAD

Etna

RUDDSBORO ROAD

KING ROAD

Enfield
Reservoir

PAVED ROAD   ©

GRAVEL ROAD

DOUBLE-TRACK TRAIL

SINGLE-TRACK TRAIL

PRIVATE, OFF-LIMITS,
OR INAPPROPRIATE
FOR BICYCLING

WETLAND   BODY OF
                 WATER

HILLTOP
OR SUMMIT   N

0   MILES   1.0

quiet, country road should be. Surrounded by a mixture of deep forest and open field, it rolls through the hills and dales below **Moose Mountain** revealing pretty scenery at every turn. As small farms dot the roadside, distant views spill across the Connecticut River Valley to Vermont. Cow bells can be heard ringing from the hills on **Dana Road**, a similar route and the starting point for the steep and winding **Moose Mountain Road**, which climbs in switchbacks for almost a mile. Trees block the view on top but it is an exhilarating coast back down.

No longer maintained for everyday travel, Hanover's Class VI roads offer an ideal network of trails which join otherwise distant places. These forgotten farm roads were once part of everyday life but are now badly deteriorated in places so conditions for bicycling can be rough. **Chandler Road** is one of the easiest since it takes a relatively flat course until its southern end, which is still maintained and drops sharply to **Ruddsboro Road**. Nearby **Corey Road** begins on a driveway opposite Dana Road and continues for a mile along a course lined by stone walls and tall trees. It is bumpy from horse hoofprints, rocks, and occasional ruts, and emerges as a wagon track in the middle of an open field on **Wolfeboro Road** with a beautiful southern vista. Identifying this endpoint can be equally difficult, but a wooden gate marks the intersection; please leave it as you find it.

Linking the picturesque, hilltop village of **Hanover Center** with Goose Pond, Wolfeboro Road takes a 6.5-mile course through some of Hanover's most remote areas. Its surface alternates between smooth gravel and rough trail. After passing Corey Road it drops to Monahan Brook, then scrambles up a badly eroded, half-mile hill to join Three Mile Road. A third of a mile to the north Wolfeboro Road resumes, narrowing to a footpath at the base of Moose Mountain and struggling up the rocky slope for a mile before reaching a notch between **North** and **South Peaks**, where the Appalachian Trail crosses. Bearing little resemblance to a road, this steep section will require some carrying.

Fortunately the descent on the other side is more gradual and after 1.5 miles Wolfeboro Road regains a smooth, gravelly finish at the base of the mountain. Continuing on the road brings a relaxing, 1.5-mile coast down to Goose Pond but agile riders should try the more challenging **North Tunis Road** which intersects after the Moose Mountain traverse. Best if ridden in the south-to-north direction, this old road is slowed by several boggy areas halfway along but makes an enjoyable, 2-mile ride down to Goose Pond Road. Much of the surrounding land forms the **Hanover Town Forest**. For easier riding **Tunis Road**, **Goss Road**, and **Enfield Mountain Road** are good choices as they roll through evergreen forests and pass small farms on the way southward to Route 4.

Driving Directions:
From Interstate 89 take Exit 18 and follow Route 120 north for 5 miles to Hanover. Turn north on Route 10 and drive for 10 miles to Lyme, then bear right at signs for Lyme Center and continue for 3 miles to the Dartmouth Skiway. Park beside the road where the pavement ends.

Bike Shops:
Omer & Bob's Sport Shop, 7 Allen St., Hanover, (603) 643-3525

Tom Mowatt Cycles, Olde Nuggett Alley, Hanover, (603) 643-5522

Tom Mowatt Cycles, 213 Mechanic St., Lebanon, (603) 448-5556

USGS Maps:
Mount Cube Quadrangle, Mascoma Quadrangle

16
Back Roads
Tamworth

Tamworth is a sleepy little town, often overlooked as visitors center their attention on the mountain peaks of Chocorua, Paugus, and Whiteface rising above. With the bustling Lakes Region to the south and popular White Mountain towns to the north, this pocket of peace and quiet is a wonderful place for an easy ride. Its unsurfaced roads visit small farms and enjoy distant views as they roll through wooded hills. An array of mountain bike routes centers on these country roads, while a few trail options add extra challenge. Graded and well-drained, they are also a good option for early season riding when other areas are still too wet.

Easy access at **Chocorua Lake** makes it a natural starting point for a ride, but plan on spending extra time to admire the scenery. The lake's dramatic setting beneath the unmistakeable stone peak of Mount Chocorua has become one of New England's most photographed scenes, and it is difficult not to stop and gaze. Chocorua was the name of an Indian chief who lived in the area in the early 1700's and is said to have met his death on the mountain's summit. A small picnic and swimming area also make this a good endpoint to a ride.

A one-lane wooden bridge leads from this wayside into the shade of the woods on **Fowler's Mill Road**, which bends gracefully beneath enormous white pines. Century-old summer homes sit beside the road. **Loring Road** branches to the left after a half-mile and climbs a small hill to meet **Philbrick Neighborhood Road**, which returns to Fowler's Mill Road for a troublefree, 3.5-mile loop from Chocorua Lake. Nearby, a network of foot trails winds through the rocky hills of the **Clark and Bolles Reserves**, an area of preserved by the Chocorua Lake Conservation Foundation. Check for possible trailhead notices regarding bicycle usage before riding on these trails.

Fowler's Mill Road continues over a low hill and descends past **Paugus Mill Road**, 3.5 miles from Chocorua Lake. This side road ends after less than a mile at a National Forest parking area, the trailhead for popular routes such as the Liberty Trail up Mount Chocorua and Paugus Trail up Mount Paugus. In addition to steep terrain, the boundary for the Sandwich Range Wilderness Area prevents bicycles from using some of these trails, but a few miles of good riding can be enjoyed on other routes. Forest Road 68 continues past the gate and accesses the Bickford Trail, which branches to the southwest, and the Bolles Trail, which follows Paugus Brook up the notch between Mounts Chocorua and Paugus.

Stretching for another 1.2 miles over gentle terrain, Fowler's Mill Road ends at **Route 113A** and the Swift River. Route 113A is a two-lane road which follows the winding course of the river down a pretty valley to the center of **Tamworth**, about 3 miles away. The **Big Pines Natural Area** is located along the road and offers a guided nature trail. A quieter alternative is the **Old Mail Road**, which takes a 2.2-mile course of rolling hills and turns high above the river. The last mile is a steady descent to **Gardner Hill Road**. Riding Fowler's Mill Road, Old Mail Road, Gardner Hill Road, Philbrick Neighborhood Road, and Loring Road makes an 11.5-mile circuit, with hillclimbs being the only challenges.

Once the private estate of Augustus Hemenway and a public preserve since 1932, **Hemenway State Forest** is home to several good trails for mountain biking. The highlight is the ride up **Great Hill**, where bicyclists must scale a steep incline to reach the open **lookout tower** on top. Only a half-mile from the parking turnout on **Great Hill Road**, the tower has a rewarding view of mountain peaks to

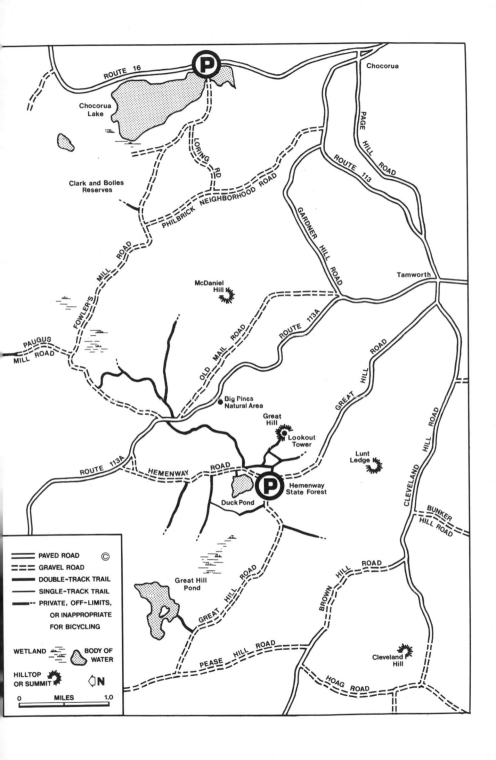

ROUTE 16

Chocorua

Chocorua
Lake

PAGE HILL ROAD

Clark and Bolles
Reserves

LORING RD

PHILBRICK NEIGHBORHOOD ROAD

ROUTE 113

GARDNER HILL ROAD

FOWLER'S MILL ROAD

McDaniel
Hill

Tamworth

PAUGUS
MILL ROAD

OLD MAIL ROAD

ROUTE 113A

GREAT HILL ROAD

Big Pines
Natural Area

Great
Hill

Lookout
Tower

Lunt
Ledge

CLEVELAND HILL ROAD

ROUTE 113A

HEMENWAY ROAD

Hemenway
State Forest

Duck Pond

BUNKER
HILL ROAD

GREAT HILL ROAD

Great Hill
Pond

BROWN HILL ROAD

PEASE HILL ROAD

Cleveland
Hill

HOAG ROAD

PAVED ROAD ©
GRAVEL ROAD
DOUBLE-TRACK TRAIL
SINGLE-TRACK TRAIL
PRIVATE, OFF-LIMITS,
OR INAPPROPRIATE
FOR BICYCLING

WETLAND   BODY OF
                 WATER

HILLTOP
OR SUMMIT   N

0   MILES   1.0

the north and Tamworth's white church steeple to the southwest.

A short, intermediate loop can be made around nearby **Duck Pond**, although the trail never sees the shoreline. Heading west on Great Hill Road, turn right on a double-track 0.3 miles from the parking turnout and follow it past an abandoned house to an open field. Cross the field and find the path continuing in the lower right corner, where it leads downhill beside a stone wall to a low point and a brief section of rocks and logs. Bear right after a half-mile where the trail intersects an old wagon road, and **Hemenway Road** is 0.3 miles ahead. Turning left on the wagon road leads westward toward **Great Hill Pond** but the blue tree blazes of the state forest boundary appear after only a quarter-mile.

Opposite Duck Pond on Hemenway Road, a marked snowmobile trail takes a downhill course to the Swift River and emerges on Route 113A near Fowler's Mill Road. It is a lively, 1.1-mile descent through pretty woodland scenery, and passes towering white pine trees whose trunks disappear above the forest canopy. The trail is smooth except for a few tree roots and is best ridden in the west-to-east direction as a steady descent. Returning to the top by the mile-long climb up Hemenway Road completes a 3-mile loop. Across the bridge on the opposite side of Route 113A the same snowmobile trail continues along Paugus Brook, passing several tempting swimming holes before emerging at Fowler's Mill Road. A bridge over the brook was built by the Ossipee Valley Snowmobile Club, which has also marked many trail intersections with signs. Two spurs diverge to the right but eventually meet private lands.

Keep in mind when parking at Hemenway State Forest that you are starting from the top of a hill, so save some energy for the return ride. Hemenway Road's mile-long ascent from Route 113A is steep in places, and Great Hill Road rises steadily for 2.6 miles from Tamworth center. Great Hill Road continues for another 2.4 miles west of the parking area, passing mountain views to the south from an open field at one point. At the 2-mile mark watch for a woods road on the right which leads to the boggy shores of **Great Hill Pond**. This is privately-owned land and the owners ask that visitors show it proper respect.

Still more gravel roads can be found to the west where the undulating terrain is reflected in the names of **Brown Hill Road** and **Pease Hill Road**. The woods give way to nice views of Mount Chocorua and other scenes at the clearings of farms and summer homes along these country roads. **Hoag Road** has a quieter feel as it explores the deep woods near **Cleveland Hill**.

Driving Directions:
Chocorua Lake is located on Route 16, 1.5 miles north of the village of Chocorua and 9 miles south of Route 112 (Kancamagus Highway). Park at the beginning of Fowler's Mill Road, before the wooden bridge.

To reach Hemenway State Forest from Route 16, turn west on Route 113 at the village of Chocorua and drive for 3 miles to a stop sign, where Route 113 turns left and Route 113A turns right. Continue straight at this intersection and drive through the center of Tamworth to Great Hill Road, on the right before the church. After 2.6 miles Great Hill Road intersects Hemenway Road where a small area provides parking.

Bike Shops:
The Bike Shop, Mountain Valley Mall Blvd., N. Conway, (603) 356-6089

Nordic Skier, 47 N. Main St., Wolfeboro, (603) 569-3151, Rentals Available

Piche's Ski & Sport Shop, Lehner St., Wolfeboro, (603) 569-8234, Rentals Available

Red Jersey Cyclery, Route 302, Glen, (603) 383-4660

Sports Outlet, Main St., N. Conway, (603) 356-3133, Rentals Available

USGS Maps:
Mount Chocorua Quadrangle, Ossipee Lake Quadrangle

17
White Mountain National Forest
Stinson Lake

Stinson Lake is a refreshingly simple place, a far cry from the bustle of other villages in the White Mountains where development has taken over the peace and quiet. The area enjoys a surprising isolation at the southern bounds of the National Forest, where a great collection of back roads, forest roads, and hiking trails explores the hilly terrain. Mountain biking opportunities abound and many well-known routes have become favorites for the student population of nearby Plymouth.

Some of the area's mountain biking routes follow town roads situated beyond the bounds of the National Forest, so remember that they are bordered by private lands. A few have Class VI designation, meaning that they are no longer maintained for regular travel but still open to public use. Also be aware that snowmobile trails crossing the area often utilize private lands under winter-only agreements, so landowners may or may not permit summer usage. Many snowmobile trails are also too rough, wet, or overgrown for enjoyable mountain biking.

The bicycling is focused in two distinct areas. Much of the riding is on the old roads and foot trails near **Stinson Lake**, where conditions are generally more challenging, while the gravel roads in the lower elevations near **Campton Bog** and **Loon Lake** provide obstacle-free alternatives. Hills are plentiful in both locations, and pedaling between them involves a major elevation change since Stinson Lake sits high in the hills and Campton Bog lies in the valley below.

Find the easiest pedaling on the gravel roads surrounding Campton Bog, where a small parking spot beside **Robartwood Pond** makes a good starting point. **Bog Road** rolls gently through the woods at the foot of the mountains, connecting with **East Rumney Road** and **Chaisson Road** for a trouble-free ride past occasional homes and small farms. Descending to the south, East Rumney Road and Chaisson Road reach an **abandoned railroad bed** which offers the area's straightest, flattest bicycling. This grade has a smooth, gravelly surface and parallels the Baker River in the open fields of the valley floor.

Nearby Class VI roads are more difficult to ride, with the northwestern end of **Craig Hill Road** suffering from erosion. Similarly, the southern portion of **Chandler Hill Road** climbs over a rough surface, passing beautiful farm fields before emerging beside an apple orchard on **Mason Road**, where a southern vista awaits. Continue for another mile up **Berry Farm Road** to enjoy a northern view across the Pemigewasset River Valley to Franconia Notch.

Banked by a ring of hills, Stinson Lake sits in a protected hollow with summer cottages dotting its shoreline. A 6-mile loop circumnavigates the lake, with the paved **Stinson Lake Road** offering the only views over the water. **Cross Road** and **Doetown Road** are both buried in the shade of forest and roll through the terrain above the lake, with rarely a car to be seen. Unfortunately there is no public place to swim at Stinson and access to the water is limited to the **boat launch** beside the Stinson Lake Store, which marks the village center.

Doetown Road continues south from Cross Road for a half-mile with smooth gravel, then becomes a Class VI road and descends with treacherous conditions toward Rumney, ending far below on Stinson Lake Road. Poorly drained and badly eroded, this 1.5-mile section of Doetown Road is a steep and challenging ride and should be ridden in the downhill (north-to-south) direction.

The **Stinson Mountain Trail** is a hiking route to the top of 2890-foot **Stinson Mountain** and leaves from a small turnout on Doetown Road. The trail begins as an old farm

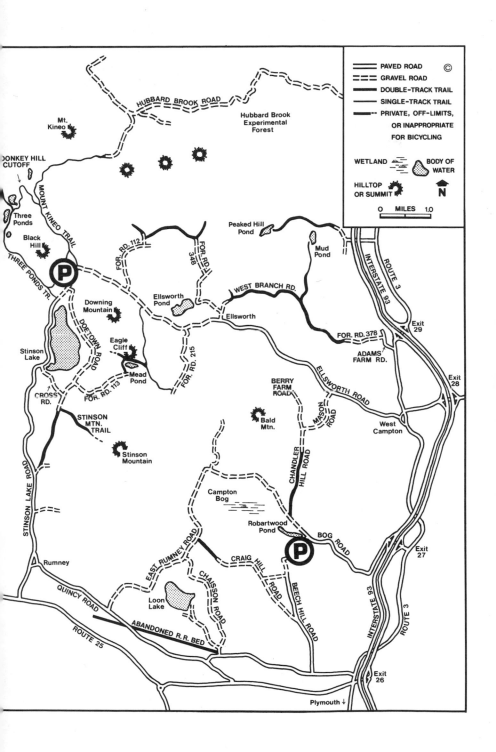

road, bumping over rocky ground in a hardwood forest and climbing gradually for the first half-mile beside stone walls. It then narrows at the remains of a granite foundation and becomes too steep for bicycling, but continues for over a mile to the summit views. Total elevation gain is 1400' from Doetown Road.

Forest Road 113 leaves Doetown Road opposite Stinson Lake. Identifiable only by its metal gate, it climbs for the first half-mile and then gently descends for a mile to a sharp, right-hand turn, where it fades. Look for a trail leading to the left on the outside of this turn and follow it across a brook to another intersection. To the left, the trail lasts for only a half-mile before leaving the National Forest, but to the right it continues through a pass marked by **Mead Pond** and the rock ledges of **Eagle Cliff**. An overgrown snowmobile trail named Poker Run forks left as the trail continues over a small hill and reduces to single-track for an exciting downhill ride. Although this section does not appear to get much foot traffic, chainring marks on logs reveal its popularity with mountain bikers. After a half-mile descent, turn left on **Forest Road 215**. Smooth but for the moose prints stamped into its surface, this gravel road stretches for a mile and a half to **Ellsworth Road**. Turn left on Ellsworth Road to return to Stinson Lake and complete a challenging, 8.5-mile loop.

The alternative way to reach Stinson Lake from below, Ellsworth Road begins at **Route 3** in **West Campton**. The first 5 miles are paved and climb steeply past several sweeping views of the White Mountains, while the remaining 3.5 miles have a gravel surface and more gradual slope. Surrounded by quiet forest, the upper end of Ellsworth Road offers a pristine ride.

Ellsworth is a village barely noticeable beside the road, and is identifiable only by a small chapel and one-room schoolhouse. A side road running downhill to **Ellsworth Pond** serves as the starting point for the **West Branch Road**, one of the area's most popular mountain biking routes. A combination of Class VI and forest service road, it descends for 4 miles beside the ledges and waterfalls of West Branch Brook, offering intermediate riding with a few wet and eroded spots. From Ellsworth the road crosses a bridge over the brook, bears right at the next fork, then enters the National Forest at 1.2 miles. An old skid road diverges left at 1.8 miles with a challenging side trip to the boggy shores of **Mud Pond**. Continuing straight, the last mile is easy riding as bicyclists cruise over the smooth, gravel surface of **Forest Road 378**. To return by pavement and complete a 10-mile loop, turn right at the end of Forest Road 378 and follow **Adams Farm Road** to Route 3. Turn right and continue for 1.3 miles to West Campton, turn right and ride up the hill, then turn right on Ellsworth Road and ride for 4.8 miles back to Ellsworth.

Forest Road 348 provides another intermediate option from Ellsworth village. Find this gated, gravel road past Ellsworth Pond on the left side, just before the dead end, and follow it uphill to a clearing where it forks into two double-tracks. Turn left, cross a snowmobile bridge, and continue for 1.5 miles. The trail then emerges at a logging road only a short distance above **Forest Road 112**, which returns with a smooth surface to Ellsworth Road.

Three Ponds Trail is an easy hike but a challenging fat-tire ride. The trail is the first leg of a difficult, 4.5-mile loop beginning and ending at the parking lot north of Stinson Lake. It stretches for 1.8 miles to **Three Ponds**, where an overnight shelter and an inspiring, hillside setting provide a good resting spot. The Three Ponds Trail starts by crossing a small ridge, bouncing over rocks and twisting around trees before crossing Sucker Brook at 0.7 miles. It then follows the brook upstream, crossing it several times and climbing steeper pitches at the sound of each waterfall. Although many sections are smooth and flat, others will require carrying.

Beyond the shelter bear right on the **Donkey Hill Cutoff** where the Three Ponds Trail turns left, continuing for

Trail and reach **Hubbard Brook Road** (Forest Road 22) after a difficult, 4-mile trip. Not only are conditions often too steep, too rocky, or too muddy for bicycling, but the trail is seldom used so fallen trees and debris obstruct the way and extensive carrying is required. Once over the **Mount Kineo** ridgeline the trail drops for a mile to a gravel spur off Hubbard Brook Road, a forest road which climbs through a small valley from Route 3 in Thornton. The smooth surface is a great relief after the obstacles endured on the Mount Kineo Trail, but bicyclists should respect the steepness of the road, which traverses 1200' in elevation over the course of 6 miles. Originating at Mirror Lake Road, the road serves the **Hubbard Brook Experimental Forest**, an area established by the Forest Service for timber study.

Driving Directions:

To reach the National Forest parking lot near Stinson Lake take Exit 26 from Interstate 93 for Routes 3A south and 25 west. Drive for 4 miles to a rotary where the two routes split, and continue on Route 25 west for 3.5 miles to the sign for Stinson Lake and Rumney Village. Turn right, continue through Rumney, past Stinson Lake, and find the trailhead parking lot on the left, 7 miles from Route 25 and a half-mile beyond the end of the pavement.

To reach the parking at Rowbartwood Pond take Exit 27 from Interstate 93 and follow Bog Road for 2.3 miles. Turn left at the pond and park at the turnout.

To reach Hubbard Brook Experimental Forest take Exit 29 and follow Route 3 north for 4.8 miles, turn left on Mirror Lake Road and drive for 1 mile to where the forest road forks left. Park beside the road, being careful not to block the gate.

Bike Shops:

The Greasey Wheel, 40 Main St., Plymouth, (603) 536-3655, Rentals Available

Rhino Bike Works, 95 Main St., Plymouth, (603) 536-3919

Riverside Cycle, 4 Riverside Dr., Ashland, (603) 968-9676

Ski Fanatics, Route 49, Campton, (603) 726-4327, Rentals Available

Waterville Valley Base Camp, Town Square, Waterville Valley, (603) 236-4666, Rentals Available

USGS Maps:

Mount Kineo Quadrangle, Rumney Quadrangle, Plymouth Quadrangle

Additional Information:

White Mountain National Forest, Pemigewasset Ranger District, RFD 3, Box 15, Route 175, Plymouth, NH 03264, Tel. (603) 536-1310

18
White Mountain National Forest
Waterville Valley

Nestled in the mountains at the end of the road, Waterville is truly an alpine town. The village sits in a bowl ringed by famous ski slopes and high summits, and is one of New Hampshire's best known, and most accessible, mountain resorts. Its hiking trails, rivers, and waterfalls have long attracted visitors with an outdoor spirit, and many of the skiers who schuss down the mountain or glide through the woods in winter now return to mountain bike in summer and enjoy the trails and terrain with a different perspective. Riding opportunities include a chairlift operation in the warmer months, a variety of loops close to town, and several longer excursions to outlying landmarks.

Waterville Valley has been a vacation destination since the 1830's, when an early settler by the name of Nathaniel Greeley operated a small hotel for summer visitors. Known simply for its clean air and pristine scenery, it attracted those interested in the simple, earthly pleasures of hiking and fishing. Although the alpine ski facilities now rank among the state's largest and modern condominiums dominate the valley floor, hundred-year-old trails still climb into the hills with unique appeal. The surrounding lands have been part of the White Mountain National Forest since 1928.

A maze of cross country ski trails blankets the area, but not all routes are open in summer. Since they were originally designed and built for use only during winter when the ground is frozen and protected from erosion, some trails are impassable during the warmer months when poor drainage leaves them bogged in water. The staff at Waterville Valley Base Camp, which serves as the cross country ski center in winter and mountain bike center in summer, advises that many are not suited for bicycling and have been roped off to prevent usage. Trails that remain open should never be ridden immediately after rainy periods. Since conditions and policies could change, be alert for signs and obey the requests.

Stop at Waterville Valley Base Camp in **Town Square** before you ride to pay the small trail maintenance fee, which is used to keep the trails cleared and bridges repaired. There the staff can offer rental mountain bikes, tickets for the chairlift at **Snow's Mountain** (open on weekends during the warm season), and the latest information on trail conditions and policies. They have stationed signs, maps, and intersection numbers along the trails for easy navigating.

Trails leave from the heart of the village, quickly delivering riders to natural environs. The **Village Trail** leaves from the door of Base Camp at **Corcoran's Pond** on an easy course beside the flow of Snow's Brook. It then meets the Mad River and continues downstream for a mile before ending at **Route 49**. Although some sections are effortlessly smooth, others are broken by roots and rocks, which make the riding intermediate. Note that at its midpoint the trail emerges beside the concrete pillars of an abandoned bridge and enters the **Waterville Campground**, tracing the paved drive to the end and reentering the woods on the right beside campsite #18.

Cross Route 49 and find the **Drake's Brook Ski Touring Trail** heading left from a small trailhead parking area. Several hiking trails as well as the ski trails of **Joe's Choice** and **Fletcher's Cascade** branch off this route at various intervals, but are too rough or wet for bicycling. After a steady, 1.3-mile climb from Route 49 on a surface firm and free of obstacles, a high point is reached at Intersection #9. The trail then rolls and turns with the contour of the mountain before dropping with **Snow's Brook Trail** to **Valley Loop**. The highlight of this descent is near

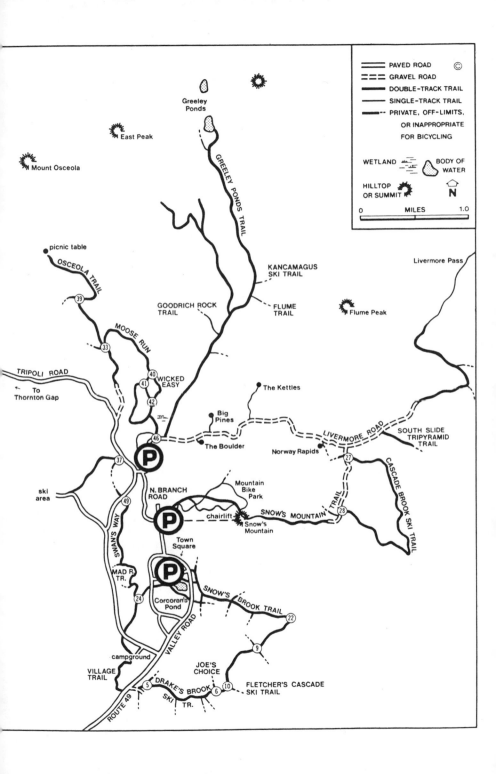

Greeley Ponds

East Peak

Mount Osceola

picnic table

OSCEOLA TRAIL

39

MOOSE RUN

33

TRIPOLI ROAD

← To
Thornton Gap

40

41

WICKED
EASY

42

46

37

ski
area

49

SWAN'S WAY

MAD R.
TR.

24

GREELEY PONDS TRAIL

KANCAMAGUS
SKI TRAIL

GOODRICH ROCK
TRAIL

FLUME
TRAIL

The Kettles

Big
Pines

The Boulder

N. BRANCH
ROAD

Mountain
Bike
Park

chairlift

Snow's
Mountain

Town
Square

Corcoran's
Pond

VALLEY ROAD

campground

VILLAGE
TRAIL

5

ROUTE 49

DRAKE'S BROOK

SKI   TR.

JOE'S
CHOICE

6   10

9

Norway Rapids

LIVERMORE ROAD

27

SNOW'S MOUNTAIN

28

SNOW'S BROOK TRAIL

22

FLETCHER'S CASCADE
SKI TRAIL

Livermore Pass

Flume Peak

SOUTH SLIDE
TRIPYRAMID
TRAIL

TRAIL

CASCADE BROOK SKI TRAIL

PAVED ROAD   ©
GRAVEL ROAD
DOUBLE-TRACK TRAIL
SINGLE-TRACK TRAIL
PRIVATE, OFF-LIMITS,
OR INAPPROPRIATE
FOR BICYCLING

WETLAND   BODY OF
                 WATER
HILLTOP
OR SUMMIT   N

0   MILES   1.0

the top where a banked, hairpin turn is a well-known crash site for skiers in winter.

The **Mad River Trail** departs the Valley Trail near **Snow's Brook Road** and crosses the Mad River near a physical fitness course. After several uphills it reaches the grassy **Swan's Way**, a flatter route which runs north for almost a mile to **Tripoli Road**. Bogged by several wet spots, Swan's Way passes through an open area of new growth forest, the result of a fierce windstorm in 1980 which blew down whole stands of trees. The tangle of deadwood was later cleared as part of a logging operation, allowing this new generation to quickly thrive.

Tripoli Road is a 10-mile route through **Thornton Gap**, a pass between Mount Tecumseh and **Mount Osceola** linking Waterville to North Woodstock. The road is paved from Waterville to the high point, where it reverts to gravel and descends past a collection of tempting forest roads and challenging foot trails. Popular camping sites can also be found. To reach the top of the pass be prepared for an uphill ride, as the road gains 700 feet in the 3 miles from the end of **West Branch Road**. Although it has been a means of reaching North Woodstock since the 1870's and it is fully passable by car, this mountain road gets minimal use and is closed each winter.

Only a half-mile up this hill **Osceola Trail** forks right on a more primitive climb on the slopes of Mount Osceola. Smooth and firm, this double-track requires a relentless effort as it rises for 1.3 miles with little relief from a constant uphill grade. The endpoint is a solitary picnic table, where the forest unfortunately blocks the view. Remember while descending that water breaks have been dug across the trail to prevent erosion and can be an unexpected hazard. **Moose Run** and **Wicked Easy** are flatter diversions off this route and are livened by plenty of stumps and sticks. Birch and hemlock trees shade the way.

The silky smooth **Livermore Road** holds some of the valley's favorite mountain biking. A gated, well-drained forest road, it passes several options for side trips as well as a string of intriguing natural features along the way. Leaving from the trailhead parking area near Depot Camp, once a logging station, the road rises at a gradual pace for 2.5 miles before degrading to a double-track trail at a small meadow, the site of another logging camp. Signs mark the intersecting trails and nearby sights like the 20-foot-tall **Boulder**, clearly evident from the road as it sits in the middle of Avalanche Brook. A short distance beyond, the Big Pines Path begins on the left and leads a quarter-mile to the four **Big Pines**, some of the area's oldest inhabitants. The **Kettles Path** is a slightly longer diversion to some impressive kettle holes, huge basins formed by the melting of glacial ice. The first part of the Kettles Path is an especially fun ride as the trail bounces and turns over a collection of small mounds, but steep hills eventually stop the bicycling before the kettles are reached. **Norway Rapids** is a unique sluiceway only a few feet from Livermore Road, but the trail bearing its name is too rough to ride.

Biking becomes more difficult after Livermore Road degrades to double-track, as rocks disrupt the surface and a few steep, eroded pitches are unrideable. After a half-mile it intersects two trails to Mount Tripyramid which are off-limits to bicycling because they enter the Sandwich Range Wilderness Area. The road then crests a ridgeline and narrows to single-track as it dips to Flume Brook and reaches **Livermore Pass**. Descending beyond this point is not recommended for biking. Returning downhill on Livermore Road's smooth gravel is a relaxing coast, but remember that others may be using the trail so stay to the right and keep to a safe speed.

Look for the **Snow's Mountain Trail** leading across a large, wooden bridge, 2.2 miles from the parking area. Beginning with an easy gravel surface, the trail winds past roaring brooks and mountain views before becoming a more challenging double-track, bouncing over bumps and scrambling up short hills. Experts should try **Cascade**

Brook Ski Trail, where a long slope, deeply gauged water bars, and plentiful rocks obstruct the way.

Riding **Greeley Ponds Trail** is a more challenging endeavor but it yields prized scenery which is well worth the effort. One of the region's oldest paths, this route through Mad River Notch dates from 1860 and was originally a means of reaching the Saco River Valley. Today it is a popular hiking and cross country skiing trail, but a difficult trip for mountain biking since riders are forced to pick an intricate course over rocks and roots. Fortunately elevation gain is minimal. After 3 miles of gradual uphill the trail splits, with the hiking path bearing left and the skiing trail continuing straight and soon ending at the first of the **Greeley Ponds**. The hiking trail continues with many carries to the second and more beautiful of the ponds deep within the walls of the notch, where Mount Kancamagus meets Mount Osceola's **East Peak** with a dramatic display of cliffs and slides. The serenity at the water's edge is a marked contrast to the struggle of the trail. Greeley Ponds is a designated Scenic Area, so camping and fires are prohibited.

A variety of trails diverge from the Greeley Ponds Trail, but most are either too steep or too overgrown for bicycling. This includes both the **Flume Trail** and the **Kancamagus Ski Trail**. The exception is an unmarked double-track which bears left shortly after the **Goodrich Rock Trail**. Obscured by forest growth, this old logging road climbs at a rideable grade to a bowl high on Mount Osceola, offering a fine view across the valley to the three summits of Mount Tripyramid and, once the leaves have fallen, another into Mad River Notch.

One of Waterville's highlights is the **Mountain Bike Park** at Snow's Mountain. With chairlift rides available on summer weekends and a variety of trails to try, mountain bikers of all abilities can avoid having to pedal uphill. While many choose to maneuver down the slopes of the ski area, others can enjoy the longer, more gradual descent on the

Snow's Mountain Trail and Livermore Road. The top of the lift offers a beautiful overlook of the valley with Mount Tecumseh in the background. Tickets can be purchased at Waterville Valley Base Camp.

Driving Directions:
From Interstate 93 take Exit 28 and follow Route 49 east for 10 miles to the village. To park at Town Square, turn left on Village Road after passing Corcoran's Pond. To park at Livermore Road, follow Valley Road to West Branch Road, turn left and the lot is less than a mile ahead on the right, just before Tripoli Road.

Bike Shops:
The Greasey Wheel, 40 Main St., Plymouth, (603) 536-3655,
Rhino Bike Works, 95 Main St., Plymouth, (603) 536-3919
Riverside Cycle, 4 Riverside Dr., Ashland, (603) 968-9676
Ski Fanatics, Route 49, Campton, (603) 726-4327, Rentals Available
Waterville Valley Base Camp, Town Square, Waterville Valley, (603) 236-4666, Rentals Available

USGS Maps:
Mount Osceola Quadrangle, Plymouth Quadrangle, Mount Chocorua Quadrangle

Additional Information:
White Mountain National Forest, Pemigewasset Ranger District, RFD 3, Box 15, Route 175, Plymouth, NH 03264, Tel. (603) 536-1310

19
White Mountain National Forest
Sandwich Notch

Hidden in the foothills above the Lakes Region, the trails of the Sandwich Range are home to some of New Hampshire's best mountain biking. They branch from a historic backcountry road in a surprisingly unspoiled wilderness, offering bicyclists deserted footpaths and an array of gravel roads. And since many routes follow sparkling mountain streams, Sandwich Notch is an especially inviting place to ride on a hot summer day.

Sandwich Notch Road was officially opened in 1801 and for a generation was the lifeblood of a small mountain community. It existed as a mere trail before that time, and eventually became an important trade route between northern Vermont and the seaport of Portland, Maine. It has changed little over the years and remains a true mountain road, winding for 11 miles on a pot-holed course through the forest, clinging to hillsides and sneaking past boulders and ledge with barely the width for a car. It is this primitive character which makes the Notch Road ideal for mountain biking. Surrounded by wilderness and wrinkled with hills and turns, it offers both the natural appeal of a trail and the ease of pedaling on firm gravel. Pavement covers a few sections where the slope threatens the road with erosion.

Bicyclists should keep in mind that the Notch Road's big uphills make the pedaling strenuous, and its narrow width and long descents deserve caution since vehicles also use the road. After a steep climb from **Route 49**, the road enjoys a mountain view before disappearing into the woods on the 2.5-mile climb to the **height of land**, 1776 feet above sea level, marked by a small metal sign on the left side. This high point gives way to a 2.5-mile descent to the Beebe

River, where a major intersection of trails is the geographical center of the area's mountain biking options, as well as a strategic place to park. From the Beebe River bridge the Notch Road continues for nearly 6 miles. It parallels the Bearcamp River for much of the way while passing cellarholes and stone walls which are reminders of the road's long history. After intersecting **Dale Road** and Dinsmore Pond Road at lower elevation, riders can coast over pavement and descend past nice views of Squam Lake to the classic, white clapboard village of **Center Sandwich.**

The Notch Road offers a good collection of side trips to make the ride more interesting. Two routes reach the shores of the **Hall Ponds**, known for great trout fishing, and a rough road climbs to scenic **Kiah Pond**. Just downhill from the **Ridgepole Trail** look for the small parking lot and footpath for **Beede Falls**, where the headwaters of the Bearcamp River spill over ledge with an impressive display. Various other jeep tracks leave the Notch Road with promising looks but eventually come to dead ends.

An easy, popular ride for mountain biking, the **Beebe River Road** is an old railroad grade and follows the flow of the river westward for 6 miles to **Eastern Corners Road** in Campton. The sound and scenery of the water make it a beautiful trip, and several picnicking spots can be found at choice locations. It also serves as the first leg of a 19-mile loop on a combination of roads and intermediate trail. Turn right on Eastern Corners Road and continue for 1.8 miles to a four-way intersection, where **Page Road** turns right. Follow this unmaintained Class VI road over a low hill to reach **Winter Brook Road** after 2.2 miles, then ride downhill to **Route 175**, turn right for **Campton**, then right again on Route 49 to return to Sandwich Notch Road, 5 miles from its intersection with the Beebe River. For a more difficult alternative, try **Chickenboro Road** which climbs over eroded areas and fords several streams to reach an unmarked forest road off the Notch Road. Note that Chickenboro Road is best ridden in the opposite direction, since it is all downhill.

The Smarts Brook Ski Trails are a small but enjoyable network for intermediate riders. They begin beside Route 49 at a marked trailhead and climb into the shady hills above the Mad River, offering pretty scenery of streams and forest along the way. The steep uphill at the beginning of the **Smarts Brook Trail** soon mellows to a gradual climb on the smooth and firm course of an old logging road. It follows the flow of Smarts Brook for the first 1.5 miles, degrades to a rocky single-track, and then enters the Sandwich Range Wilderness Area, where bicycles are prohibited. Return down the hill on the intermediate **Yellow Jacket Trail**, which leaves Smarts Brook as a single-track, dips through several wet areas, then widens and flattens before meeting **Old Waterville Road**, a 2-mile piece of wagon track that was once the main route up the valley. The **Pine Flat Trail** has a nice cushion of needles and enjoys a dramatic view over a small gorge carved by a stream. It combines with the Smarts Brook and Yellow Jacket trails to form a 3.3-mile loop. The rough-hewn **Trl-Town Trail** and **Atwood Loop Trail** are both overgrown ski routes with difficult riding conditions, and connect to Sandwich Notch Road.

Dickey Notch is a more challenging destination and meant only for experts. After starting at the end of **Orris Road** and rising gradually for a mile as a smooth double-track, the **Dickey Notch Trail** passes a series of beaver ponds and begins a difficult climb with rocks, transitions, and undoubtedly some carrying. It reaches a high point between **Cone Mountain** and the bald, granite faces of **Dickey** and **Welch Mountains**, then descends to a forest road at the end of Mill Brook Road in Thornton.

Another ride recommended for ambitious cyclists is the 8-mile trip to **Flat Mountain Pond**. The ride begins as an easy cruise but gets progressively more difficult, with several carries required near the end. The first leg is the **Guinea Pond Trail**, which leaves the Notch Road just uphill from the Beebe River bridge and scrambles up a slope to

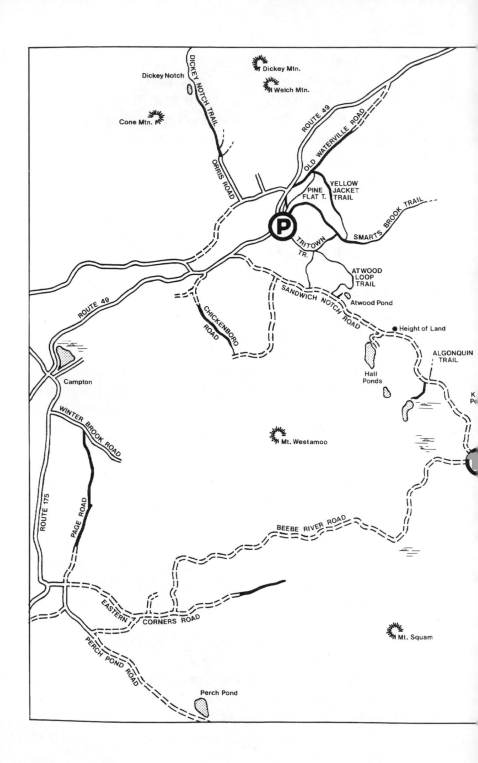

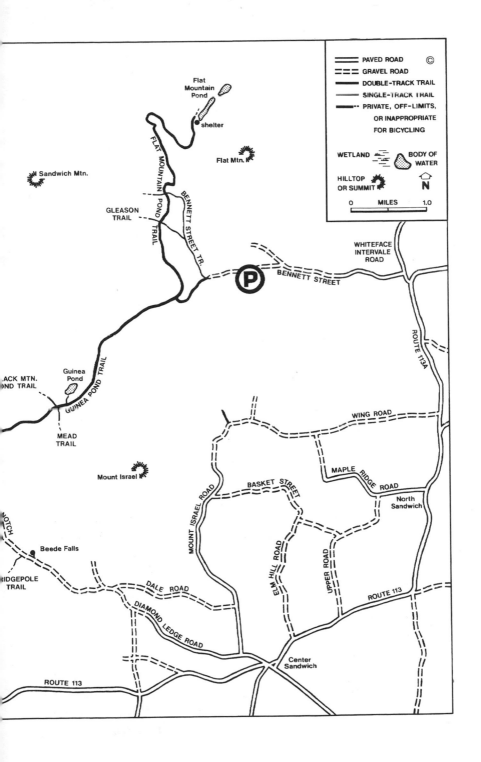

Flat
Mountain
Pond

shelter

PAVED ROAD   ©
GRAVEL ROAD
DOUBLE-TRACK TRAIL
SINGLE-TRACK TRAIL
PRIVATE, OFF-LIMITS,
OR INAPPROPRIATE
FOR BICYCLING

WETLAND   BODY OF
               WATER
HILLTOP
OR SUMMIT   N

0   MILES   1.0

Flat Mtn.

Sandwich Mtn.

FLAT MOUNTAIN POND TRAIL

BENNETT STREET TR.

GLEASON
TRAIL

WHITEFACE
INTERVALE
ROAD

P

BENNETT STREET

ROUTE 113A

Guinea
Pond

GUINEA POND TRAIL

WING ROAD

ACK MTN.
ND TRAIL

MAPLE RIDGE ROAD

MEAD
TRAIL

North
Sandwich

Mount Israel

MOUNT ISRAEL ROAD

BASKET STREET

NOTCH

Beede Falls

ELM HILL ROAD

UPPER ROAD

RIDGEPOLE
TRAIL

DALE ROAD

ROUTE 113

DIAMOND LEDGE ROAD

Center
Sandwich

ROUTE 113

join the course of the railroad grade along the Beebe River, where it is predictably smooth and flat. The easy rolling is interrupted by isolated wet spots, eroded areas, and stream gullies, as well as single-track detours around two beaver flowages. At 1.6 miles the **Black Mountain Pond Trail** and **Mead Trail** depart to ascend nearby peaks and a nearby spur leads to the boggy shores of **Guinea Pond**.

Four miles from Sandwich Notch Road the Guinea Pond Trail ends at the **Flat Mountain Pond Trail**. Turn right to descend the steep logging road and reach a parking area at the end of **Bennett Street**, or continue straight for another 3.8 miles to Flat Mountain Pond. Beware that this portion of the railroad grade follows the boundary of the Sandwich Range Wilderness Area, so bicycles are prohibited from all routes west of the Flat Mountain Pond Trail and those beyond Flat Mountain Pond. The riding along this segment is gradual uphill, disrupted by occasional rocky areas and a brief series of embedded railroad ties. The bridges which once spanned the streams are long gone, so steep gullies remain. Close to the pond the hills get bigger and only the most skilled bicyclist will reach its beautiful scenery without walking some sections.

Both the **Bennett Street Trail** and **Gleason Trail** east of the Flat Mountain Pond Trail are open to bicycling and offer a scenic option for a return trip along Pond Brook. Although both trails initially drop down unrideable slopes, they flatten upon reaching the brook and follow the flow as it rushes over polished rocks and spills into idyllic pools. Best taken in the north-to-south direction, the trails are a technical rider's dream of close quarters and careful maneuvers.

A series of back roads runs north from Center Sandwich with trouble-free riding, and offer another loop variation. From the Bennett Street parking lot find **Wing Road** 2 miles south on **Route 113A**, with a gravel surface which eventually narrows as it heads uphill. At the top **Maple Ridge Road** descends to the left to reach the small settlement of **North Sandwich**. Continuing straight, **Mt. Israel Road** rolls with big ups and downs, exposing mountain views at a few points and arcing southward beneath **Mount Israel**, where pavement resumes. Combining the Guinea Pond Trail with Bennett Street, Route 113A, Mt. Israel Road, Dale Road, and Sandwich Notch Road creates a 20-mile loop. Other scenic routes include **Basket Street** and **Elm Hill Road**, which have moderately hilly courses and join at the Bearcamp River.

Driving Directions:
From Interstate 93, take Exit 28 and follow Route 49 for 4.2 miles to Sandwich Notch Road, turn right and look for roadside parking at trailheads. Ample space exists by the Beebe River, 5 miles from Route 49.

The Smarts Brook trailhead is located on Route 49, 5.5 miles from Interstate 93.

To reach the Bennett Street trailhead, follow Route 113 from Center Sandwich to North Sandwich, then bear left on Route 113A toward Wonalancet. Turn left on Whiteface Intervale Road after 3 miles from North Sandwich, then immediately left on Bennett Street. Bear left at the next fork and find the trailhead parking at the end.

Bike Shops:
The Greasey Wheel, 40 Main St., Plymouth, (603) 536-3655
Rhino Bike Works, 95 Main St., Plymouth, (603) 536-3919
Riverside Cycle, 4 Riverside Dr., Ashland, (603) 968-8234
Ski Fanatics, Route 49, Campton, (603) 726-4327, Rentals Available
Waterville Valley Base Camp, Town Square, Waterville Valley, (603) 236-4666, Rentals Available

USGS Maps:
Plymouth Quadrangle, Mount Chocorua Quadrangle

Additional Information:
White Mountain National Forest, Pemigewasset Ranger District, RFD 3, Box 15, Route 175, Plymouth, NH 03264, Tel. (603) 536-1310

20
White Mountain National Forest
North Conway

The famous factory outlet shopping centers are not the only attraction to North Conway, which also has a well-deserved reputation for the outdoors. Surrounded by mountains for hiking, rivers for canoeing, cliffs for rock climbing, and acres of beautiful woodlands with trails ideal for mountain biking, the town is a paradise for outdoor adventure. While its paved roads might be snarled with traffic, mountain bicyclists can roll freely over nearby forest roads and footpaths.

North Conway's strong tourist appeal does warrant a word of caution. Trails that lead to unique sights and natural places can be busy with people, especially on summer weekends, so be sensitive to the heavy usage. Always yield trail to hikers and pedal extra softly at popular areas. Also note that parking can be found at many trailheads in addition to the locations shown on the map.

The trailhead parking lot for the **Mineral Site Trail** is a good starting point for exploring the area's backcountry bicycling. The Mineral Site Trail is a newly-created single-track which dances around stumps and rolls over bumps for a lively ride. After 1 mile it reaches the **Mineral Collecting Site**, marked by a sign, where visitors are invited to search for quartz amid the mounds of prior attempts. The trail then widens to double-track and descends steadily for 0.7-miles to **Forest Road 379**. The Collecting Site is a popular attraction so be prepared to encounter foot traffic along the way.

Forest Road 380 is a smoother route down to Forest Road 379. Descending from **High Street** in a series of steep pitches, it curves through an alternating pattern of undisturbed forest and devastated clearcuts, where wild raspberries scent the summer air. Combining Mineral Site Trail, Forest Road 379, and Forest Road 380 yields an intermediate, 5.5-mile ride. The loop is best ridden in the clockwise direction.

Forest Road 379 is one of the area's best mountain biking routes as it leads far into the back woods. The road stretches for a total of 4.5 miles before dead-ending, with sizeable hills being the only challenge. It begins at Cedar Creek Development on **West Side Road**, 2.7 miles south of **River Road** and 2.8 miles north of **Passaconnaway Road**. Flat terrain and the road's smooth, gravel finish ensure easy pedaling for the first 2 miles to Forest Road 380. The road then takes a sweeping turn to the left and begins an arduous, 2.5-mile climb to an area of clearcuts, where the open space allows a view of the **North**, **Middle**, and **South Moat Mountains**. These summits were named for the abundant beaver flowages which once blocked their streams. Several trails diverge from Forest Road 379 but eventually leave the national forest for private property.

The **Red Ridge Trail** is the exception to this, and makes for a demanding ride. West of Forest Road 379 the trail climbs to the Moat Mountains and should not be attempted, but east of the road it provides a manageable for experienced bicyclists. The surface is frequently broken by long sections of rocks and roots and will require some carrying. It extends for 1.4 miles, crossing several faint skid roads before ending at Lucy Brook and **Moat Mountain Trail**. Turn right and descend for a half-mile to the popular swimming hole at **Diana's Baths**, where clear pools sit beneath a series of waterfalls. Note that swimming is prohibited above the falls, where water supply intake pipes are located. Parking is available at the Moat Mountain trailhead on West Side Road.

Halfway along, a spur from Red Ridge Trail scales a steep hill to reach **White Horse Ledge**. The trail is too steep for bicycling but the half-mile hike to the top provides

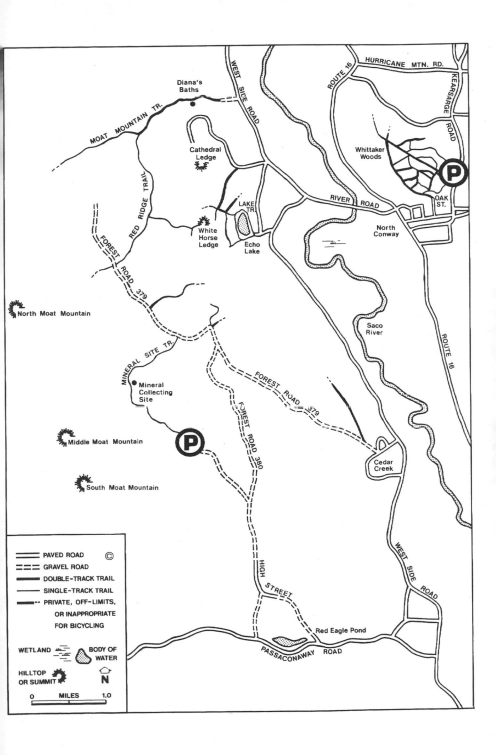

HURRICANE MTN. RD.

ROUTE 16

KEARSARGE ROAD

Diana's
Baths

MOAT MOUNTAIN TR.

WEST SIDE ROAD

Whittaker
Woods

P

OAK
ST.

Cathedral
Ledge

RED RIDGE TRAIL

RIVER ROAD

North
Conway

LAKE
TR.

White
Horse
Ledge

Echo
Lake

FOREST ROAD 379

North Moat Mountain

Saco
River

ROUTE 16

MINERAL SITE TR.

Mineral
Collecting
Site

FOREST ROAD 379

Middle Moat Mountain

P

FOREST ROAD 380

Cedar
Creek

South Moat Mountain

WEST SIDE ROAD

HIGH STREET

Red Eagle Pond

PASSACONAWAY ROAD

PAVED ROAD   ©

GRAVEL ROAD

DOUBLE-TRACK TRAIL

SINGLE-TRACK TRAIL

PRIVATE, OFF-LIMITS,
OR INAPPROPRIATE
FOR BICYCLING

WETLAND   BODY OF
                WATER

HILLTOP
OR SUMMIT   N

0   MILES   1.0

a bird's eye view of the farm fields in the valley of the **Saco River**. Named for a light-colored patch resembling the image of a horse, the open cliff face has a verticle drop of several hundred feet and is a renowned playground for rock climbers. To the north, a 1.5-mile paved road climbs neighboring **Cathedral Ledge** from West Side Road for a similar view.

Echo Lake State Park sits beneath these towering cliffs with a broad, sandy beach and a much more relaxed atmoshere. A few miles of mellow trails surround the water, with the **Lake Trail** making a 1-mile loop along the shoreline. Roots make it a bumpy, intermediate ride in places but other trails branch off along the way with smoother riding. Parking is available at Echo Lake but a fee is charged.

Closer to town is an area of Conway Conservation Land known as **Whittaker Woods**, where a small oasis of trails offers a variety of escape routes from the bustling shops on Main Street, only a few hundred yards away. Frequent intersections and a lack of signs can make this dense network confusing at times, but the area is confined to a small size and the forest of tall trees is a beautiful place to get lost. Beware that the proximity to town means that these trails are busy with walkers, runners, and horseback riders so plan on slow speeds and be extra sensitive about your impact on the trail surface.

Most trails at Whittaker Woods are double-track but not all are easy to pedal, since steep inclines abound. A hill centered on the property affects most of the trails and provides a few viewpoints. From the parking lot on **Kearsarge Road**, follow the open corridor of the powerlines over a hill as it extends for a mile to a set of railroad tracks. Many other trails intersect along this course. Turn left at the base of the hill before the tracks and follow the peaceful woods road as it meanders through a quiet forest of tall pines. The trail extends for 0.6 miles to **Oak Street**, where it is possible to return to the parking lot via Mechanic and

Kearsarge Streets for a 2.2-mile loop. A more difficult option is on the northern side of the powerlines, where a rough-hewn ski trail presents a challenging array of logs and stumps.

Driving Directions:
To reach the Mineral Collecting Site trailhead parking, take West Side Road north from Route 16 in Conway. After 1 mile turn left on Passaconaway Road, continue for 1.2 miles, and turn right on High Street. Park at the end of the road. Coming from North Conway, take River Road to West Side Road and continue south for 5.5 miles to Passaconaway Road, then as above.

To reach Whittaker Woods, follow Kearsarge Street from downtown North Conway. Find the parking area on the left where a set of powerlines crosses the road.

Bike Shops:
The Bike Shop, Mountain Valley Mall Blvd., N. Conway, (603) 356-6089

Joe Jones Ski & Sports, Main St., N. Conway, (603) 356-9411, Rentals Available

Red Jersey Cyclery, Route 302, Glen, (603) 383-4660

Sports Outlet, Main St., N. Conway, (603) 356-3133, Rentals Available

USGS Maps:
North Conway Quadrangle

Additional Information:
White Mountain National Forest, Saco Ranger District, RFD 1, Box 94, Kancamagus Highway, Conway, NH 03818, Tel. (603) 447-5448

21
White Mountain National Forest
Bear Notch

Located in the heart of the White Mountains, the Bear Notch area is home to some of the National Forest's most extensive mountain biking. A vast collection of trails and backcountry roads unfolds over a wilderness of peacefully flowing streams and challenging mountain slopes. With many day-long excursions and plenty of nearby campgrounds, it makes an ideal weekend getaway.

Before starting a ride in the White Mountains remember to be prepared for the worst. The Bear Notch region is large and some of the routes described are very isolated, so help is far away. Ride with a companion, carry water, food, and bike tools, and be ready for abrupt weather changes, even in summer.

Bear Notch Road lies at the center of the area's mountain biking options. A paved, two-lane road connecting the famous **Kancamagus Highway** (Route 112) with **Route 302**, Bear Notch Road is 9 miles long and straddles the ridgeline which separates the **Saco River** from the **Swift River**. It climbs a relentless slope to the highpoint at **Bear Notch**, gaining 600 feet of elevation from the Kancamagus before descending with a long coast. Spectacular mountain scenery makes it a rewarding ride, but cyclists should use caution. Similar to the popular bicycle route over neighboring Kancamagus Pass, Bear Notch Road can be busy with cars and camping vehicles on summer weekends. It is also rippled with frost heaves in places.

The **Bartlett Experimental Forest** sits on the northern side of Bear Notch above the village of **Bartlett** with a maze-like, 8-mile network of easy and intermediate gravel roads buried in the shade of dense woods. The

2600-acre area has been set aside by the Forest Service as a field laboratory for the study of timber growth, disease response, and logging techniques. Beware upon entering the Experimental Forest that there are no signs or landmarks for navigating and each road begins to look the same. Bring a map and pay careful attention to it. Though smooth, many of the roads cling to steep hillsides, including **Haystack Road** which takes a 3-mile trip to the Notch Road's high point. Other trails explore the woods on the opposite side of the Notch Road with more challenging riding.

South of Bear Notch is an area of mild terrain where a variety of trails provide ideal mountain biking conditions. A marked cross country ski route, the **Lower Nanamocomuck Ski Trail** is highly recommended for intermediate-level riding and can be combined with the Kancamagus Highway for a relatively flat, 14-mile trip, complete with an optional cut-off at the half-way point. A sign marks the start of the trail at the Bear Notch Road parking area, one mile from the Kancamagus. The nearby **Paugus Trail**, also marked as Forest Road 209, ends at the Nanamocomuck and offers a smoother way to start this ride but involves a half-mile hill climb. The two routes join after a mile and tag along the banks of Swift River, which meanders around broad, sand beaches at a pace defying its name. The waters do speed up as they approach **Rocky Gorge**, a deep chasm carved through ledge where a footbridge spans the river for the short-cut option at 3.8 miles. Avoid the footpath circling nearby Falls Pond as it is often busy with hikers. Below the gorge the Nanamocomuck widens before meeting the end of **Deer Brook Road**, which continues downstream with smooth gravel for almost a mile. After 6.5 miles riders emerge at the historic **Albany Covered Bridge**, built across the Swift in 1858 and still in use. It is an 8-mile ride by road to return to the starting point.

Two side trails are encountered along the way, and both have hills demanding extra energy. The **Wenonah** and

Wenunchus Loops are both 1-mile excursions from the course, and good options for stronger pedalers in a group or for a return trip variation. Beware that the ground is littered with sticks which can easily snarl a derailleur.

The **Upper Nanamocomuck Ski Trail** gets much less use during the summer months and is a rough-hewn, difficult ride. Although some sections overlap with well-used hiking trails, others get little if any use after the snow melts so expect overgrowing brush, crude log bridges, and exposed stumps to be constant disruptions. The course is clearly marked with blue diamonds as it stretches for 10 miles between Bear Notch Road and Lily Pond.

Halfway along, **Church Pond Trail** makes a difficult, 2-mile loop from the Upper Nanamocomuck with technical riding for much of the way. Boardwalks bridge some wet areas but extensive bogs slow the pedaling. At its midpoint the trail passes a small knoll above **Church Pond**, allowing a pretty view over the water. For an easier ride, try the **Rob Brook Trail** which diverges from the Nanamocomuck to follow the grade of an old logging railway. In a few places railroad ties remain in the ground and obstruct the riding, but the trail is otherwise very flat and straight. It follows the course of Rob Brook and fords the stream several times since the railroad's bridges no longer remain.

Easier riding can be enjoyed on **Forest Road 35**, where smooth gravel penetrates deep into the forest. Gated at the Bear Notch Road parking area, it rolls and turns for 9 miles without a sign of civilization, intersecting many trails before emerging on the banks of the Swift River where it is known as **Church Pond Road**. From this terminus it is possible to wade across the river and follow a footpath for a half-mile to the Kancamagus Highway, but only when water levels permit.

The 6-mile **Sawyer Pond Trail** is a popular hiking route and a very challenging mountain bike ride. From the Swift River, bicyclists have an intermediate ride over the first 2 miles to Forest Road 35 and then begin a steady, half-mile

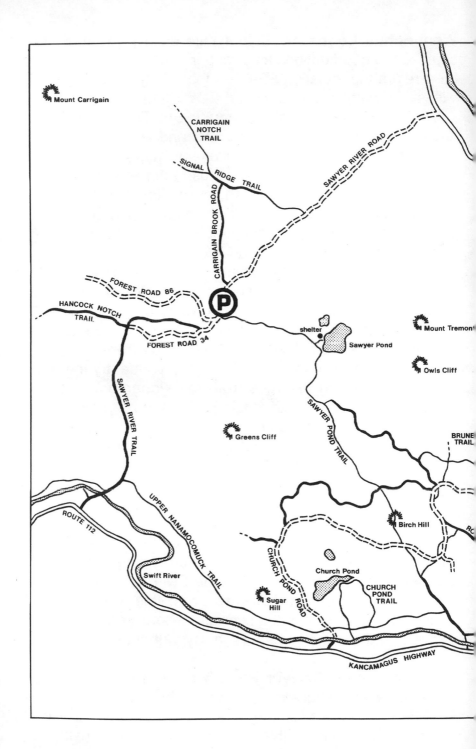

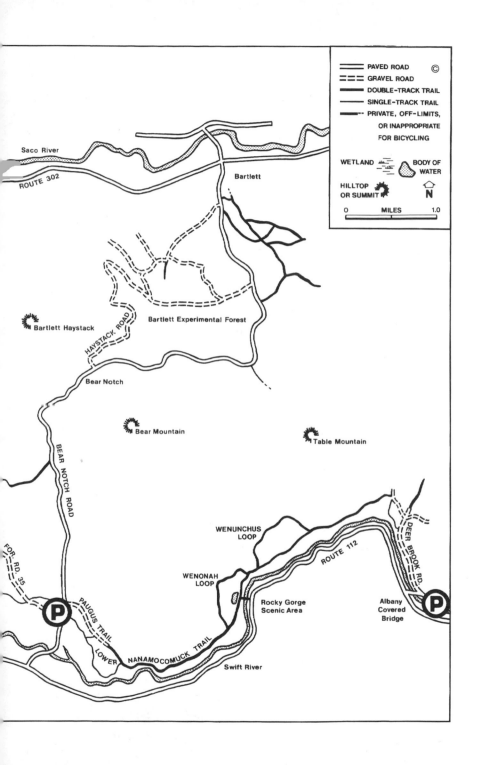

PAVED ROAD ©
GRAVEL ROAD
DOUBLE-TRACK TRAIL
SINGLE-TRACK TRAIL
PRIVATE, OFF-LIMITS,
OR INAPPROPRIATE
FOR BICYCLING

WETLAND   BODY OF
            WATER

HILLTOP   N
OR SUMMIT

0   MILES   1.0

Saco River

ROUTE 302

Bartlett

Bartlett Haystack

HAYSTACK ROAD

Bartlett Experimental Forest

Bear Notch

Bear Mountain

Table Mountain

BEAR NOTCH ROAD

WENUNCHUS
LOOP

ROUTE 112

DEER BROOK RD.

FOR. RD. 35

WENONAH
LOOP

Rocky Gorge
Scenic Area

Albany
Covered
Bridge

P

PAUGUS TRAIL

LOWER NANAMOCOMUCK TRAIL

Swift River

P

climb over **Birch Hill** with much rockier conditions. The trail descends the hill, crosses a snowmobile route, and continues with difficult conditions and many carries. At 4.5 miles the beautiful scenery of **Sawyer Pond** and **Owl's Cliff** is a welcome sight after the hard-fought struggle from the Kancamagus. A **shelter** and several tent platforms make it a possible overnight stop.

Laced with tree roots, the Sawyer Pond Trail continues for another 1.5 miles, descending to a footbridge across the Sawyer River and ending at a trailhead parking lot on **Sawyer River Road** (Forest Road 34). Sawyer River Road starts far below at the Saco River and Route 302, 4 miles west of the village of Bartlett, and climbs for 4 miles on a firm gravel surface. The road is cut into the hillside above the Sawyer River for a dramatic ride and passes two trails which climb westward toward Mount Carrigain. The unmarked **Carrigain Brook Road** is the smoothest option, though its grassy surface is offset by steep hills and a stream crossing. After 1.7 miles, it intersects the well-worn **Signal Ridge Trail**, the alternate route from Sawyer River Road and a popular one with hikers. The **Carrigain Notch Trail** can be ridden for a short distance but steep terrain eventually slows progress.

More great pedaling lies beyond the gate at the parking area. **Forest Road 86** branches to the right only to fade after 2 miles, while the Sawyer River Road continues for another 1.5 miles and links several other bike routes. A 1-mile segment of the **Sawyer River Trail** diverges right, just past a bridge over the Sawyer River, and follows another of the area's abandoned railroads once used to haul timber. Although it appears to be a temptingly smooth ride alongside the polished rocks and soothing flow of the river, an eroded section of exposed rocks requires a carry.

Sawyer River Road continues through open areas with nice mountain views before ending at a four-way intersection with Sawyer River Trail and **Hancock Notch Trail**. Starting as a double-track and gradually narrowing to a footpath, Hancock Notch Trail is peppered with rocky sections and crosses the Sawyer River several times before becoming too steep to pedal after 1.5 miles. The Sawyer River Trail proceeds on the flat railroad bed for 2.5 miles to the Kancamagus Highway, but is occasionally bumpy from tree roots. At the end the Swift River must be waded, which can be difficult at high water. The combined circuit of Sawyer Pond Trail, Sawyer River Trail, and the Kancamagus forms a challenging, 15-mile ride.

Campgrounds abound along the Kancamagus Highway, and the Passaconaway and Jigger Johnson areas are linked to the above-mentioned trails. They are apt to be full on summer weekends, so call ahead.

Driving Directions:
From Interstate 93 take Exit 32 and follow Route 112 (Kancamagus Highway) east for 23 miles. Turn left on Bear Notch Road and find the small trailhead parking area 1 mile ahead. Be careful not to block the gate.

Parking is also available at the Albany Covered Bridge, located on Route 112, 7 miles east of Bear Notch Road and 6 miles west of Route 16, and at the end of Sawyer River Road, which leaves Route 302 about 4 miles west of Bartlett.

Bike Shops:
The Bike Shop, Mountain Valley Mall Blvd., N. Conway, (603) 356-6089

Joe Jones Ski & Sports, Main St., N. Conway, (603) 356-9411, Rentals Available

Red Jersey Cyclery, Route 302, Glen, (603) 383-4660

Sports Outlet, Main St., N. Conway, (603) 356-3133, Rentals Available

USGS Maps:
Mount Chocorua Quadrangle, Crawford Notch Quadrangle

Additional Information:
White Mountain National Forest, Saco Ranger District, Kancamagus Highway, Conway, NH 03818, Tel. (603) 447-5448

22
White Mountain National Forest
Jackson

Jackson has earned a national reputation as a cross country ski resort, and proclaims itself to be the largest ski trail network in New England. Although many of the routes close to town are not open to bicycling, mountain bicyclists have more than enough options in outlying roads and trails. Some explore the stream valleys dividing the surrounding mountains while others take on the higher elevations to reach gorgeous viewpoints. Wherever you choose to ride, Jackson's friendly atmosphere and picturesque setting will make you glad you came.

Approximately 65-percent of the town lies within the bounds of the White Mountain National Forest, but not all trails are on public property. Many of the cross country skiing routes cross private lands under winter-only agreements, and landowners may or may not welcome bicyclists in summer. Be alert for the National Forest boundaries (blazed in red) and get permission before riding on private trails. Mountain bikes are not welcome on the heavily-traveled Ellis River Trail paralleling **Route 16** north of town because some parts are vulnerable to erosion and others are outside the National Forest. In addition, some ski routes get little use in the off-season and become overgrown with tall grass and weeds, so the riding is difficult.

Many of Jackson's quiet, public roads are ideal for bicycling and offer inspiring views of the mountain scenery, including the summit of Mount Washington. Both paved and unpaved, these roads depart the village in all directions to rise through the hills, and can provide an ideal ride close to town or a good warm-up for outlying trails. **Thorn Hill Road** and **Dundee Road** meander past grand old inns, cozy second homes, and farm fields with sweeping views while carrying travelers over opposite sides of **Thorn Mountain**. Another popular ride is **Route 16B** which makes a 5-mile circuit above the village center. It passes **Black Mountain Ski Area** and the popular **Jackson Falls**, where you can soak your feet in gorgeous pools, sunbath on polished slabs of ledge, and gaze off to distant mountains all at the same time.

Riders looking farther afield have many choices to make. A popular trip is to take **Carter Notch Road** and **Wildcat Valley Trail** up to one of the area's best viewpoints, **Hall's Ledge**. Parking is available at the end of the road if you prefer not to bike up the 4.5 miles from town, but many riders enjoy the challenge of starting at the village and tackling a total of 2,000 feet of elevation. The grassy Wildcat Valley Trail continues straight ahead from the road's end with a steady, 1.5-mile climb and no downhills to relieve the strain. Ancient skid roads and overgrown ski trails diverge but signs point the way to the ledge, where a picnic table awaits with a fantastic view of Mount Washington and the valley of the **Ellis River**. Halfway along sits the gigantic **Baker Memorial Rock** with a plaque recognizing the gift of the surrounding 500-acre Wildcat Reservation to the town of Jackson.

A flatter option is **Forest Road 233**, which departs at a ninety-degree angle from the end of Carter Notch Road. It extends for 2 miles over smooth gravel and mellow hills, passing several brooks and more mountain views. The **Wildcat River Trail** and **Bog Brook Trail** are difficult to notice from this road and even harder to ride, as a constant flow of roots and rocks requires expert mountain biking skills.

Town Hall Road begins near the **Saco River** and climbs beside the East Branch, losing its pavement after 2.5 miles and reaching the National Forest boundary one mile beyond. **Slippery Brook Road** continues the ascent for 4 more miles before a gate blocks traffic near the parking area for **Mountain Pond**. Continue past the gate for an enjoyable, intermediate mountain bike ride made challenging by hill climbs, some areas of loose surface, and many water breaks dug across the trail. After 2 miles the road intersects **Slippery Brook Trail** for the second time, crosses Slippery Brook on a wooden bridge, and then climbs steeply to an open meadow with a distant view. The Slippery Brook Trail, unmarked and barely noticeable near the bridge, is for advanced riders only and should be ridden in the downstream (north-to-south) direction. The trail offers a good mix of conditions, with some areas being smooth and others laced with roots and rocks. The easiest riding is toward the bottom.

More trails can be found off **East Branch Road**, which stretches for 3.5 miles to the site of a missing bridge over the East Branch of the Saco River, where a deep pool forms a perfect swimming hole. A classic backcountry road, **Black Brook Road** departs on the left behind a gate before this terminus and combines strenuous ups with exhilarating downs on a lonely course through some of the region's most remote mountain biking territory. Only a few trails intersect the 4.5 miles to the unmarked **East Branch Trail**, where the road bears right and descends into a logged clearcut, 1.5 miles from the second wooden bridge. A difficult option for returning to East Branch Road, this trail is narrow and forces tight corners, careful timing, and many carries. It passes the end of East Branch Road after 3 miles, crosses it after another 1.2 miles, then continues for 2.2 miles down to Slippery Brook Road. Several river crossings are required in the middle section but should not be attempted at high water. The terrain is flat for much of the way because the trail follows the grade of an old logging railroad, recognizeable from long, straight corridors and occasionally disruptive railroad ties. In other areas it is a narrow catwalk cut into the slope above the river and requires advanced riding skills. The East Branch is a captivating backdrop to the last segment as it slips between polished boulders into

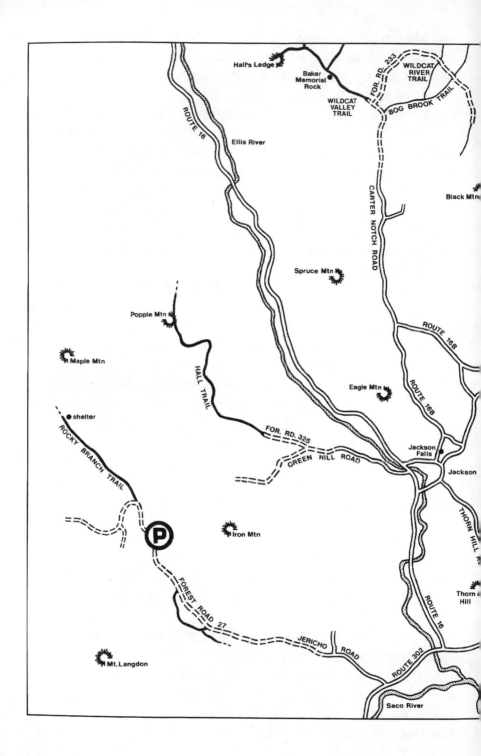

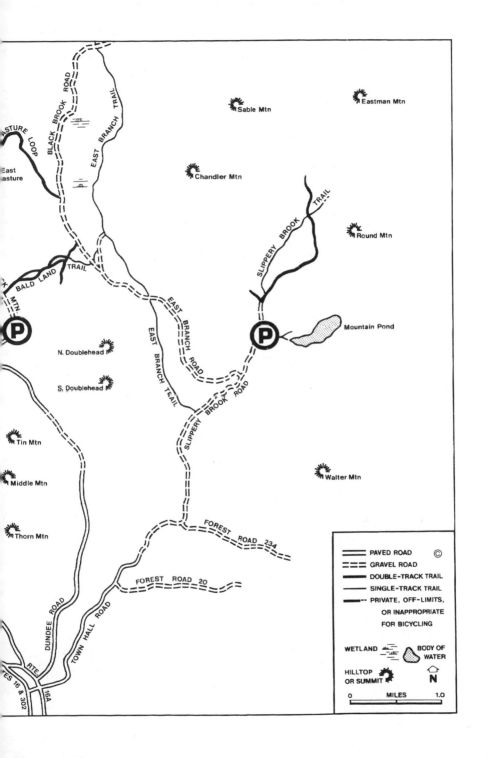

ASTURE LOOP

BLACK BROOK ROAD

EAST BRANCH TRAIL

East asture

Sable Mtn

Eastman Mtn

Chandler Mtn

SLIPPERY BROOK TRAIL

Round Mtn

BALD LAND TRAIL

K MTN.

P

EAST BRANCH ROAD

EAST BRANCH TRAIL

P

Mountain Pond

N. Doublehead

S. Doublehead

SLIPPERY BROOK ROAD

Tin Mtn

Walter Mtn

Middle Mtn

Thorn Mtn

FOREST ROAD 234

FOREST ROAD 20

DUNDEE ROAD

TOWN HALL ROAD

RTE

ES 16 & 302

16A

	PAVED ROAD	©

====== GRAVEL ROAD

────── DOUBLE-TRACK TRAIL

────── SINGLE-TRACK TRAIL

──·· PRIVATE, OFF-LIMITS,
OR INAPPROPRIATE
FOR BICYCLING

WETLAND

BODY OF
WATER

HILLTOP
OR SUMMIT

N

0   MILES   1.0

idyllic pools.

Black Mountain Road is the gateway to several trails linking Black Brook Road. It leaves Dundee Road above Black Mountain Ski Area and rises for a half-mile before becoming a Class VI road, no longer maintained but still publicly owned. A parking area at this point offers a good starting point for the **East Pasture Loop**, a 7.5-mile circuit of intermediate-level riding and a well-known trip for cross country skiers in winter. The loop is clearly marked at intersections and is equally enjoyable taken in either direction. Continue up the steady grade of Black Mountain Road on the slope of **Black Mountain**, pass through Hazelton Pasture and then enter the National Forest after a couple of miles. Reduced to a double-track, the trail intersects a path to Black Mountain Cabin at the highpoint 3 miles from the parking area, then reaches the small meadow of **East Pasture**, an appealing sight in the endless forest. A 2-mile descent to Black Brook Road follows, beginning with a steep drop and continuing with a long, gradual coast. Turn right at the road and watch for the next double-track on the right, three-quarters of a mile ahead, to continue the loop. It climbs briefly, then crests and meets **Bald Land Trail**, which returns to Black Mountain Road with a mild mix of bumps, obstacles, and wet areas.

While most of Jackson's mountain biking stretches to the east, two good routes head west. **Popple Mountain** is a 9-mile round-trip from town and requires intermediate riding skills. Begin on **Green Hill Road** and pedal uphill to a fork, two-tenths of a mile beyond the end of pavement. Bear right on **Forest Road 325** which rolls on an even course for almost a mile to a metal gate. The **Hall Trail** continues from this point, climbing steeply for the first half-mile and then rising more gradually, and intersecting several overgrown cross country ski trails along the way. After 2.5 miles it reaches the crest of Popple Mountain, where an open bog allows a partial view of Mount Washington. It is possible to descend the other side to the Rocky Branch Trailhead on

Route 16, but the biking is very difficult.

An easier ride can be enjoyed along the Rocky Branch River, where **Jericho Road** and **Forest Road** 27 travel up a small valley to the trailhead parking lot for the **Rocky Branch Trail**. Following what was once the Rocky Branch Railroad, built in 1908 to haul timber from the forests, the trail is a smooth and straight journey interrupted only by a few stream crossings and one sizeable hill. Bicycles are prohibited beyond the **shelter** 1.5 miles up the trail, where the boundary for the Presidential Range Dry River Wilderness Area is crossed. Wilderness Areas are designated by the National Forest as places to be kept in their primitive state, open only to non-mechanized uses.

Driving Directions:

The village of Jackson is located on Route 16, 2.3 miles north of Route 302. To reach Black Mountain Road follow Route 16B for 2 miles to Black Mountain Ski Area, then continue uphill on Dundee Road past the base lodge. Turn left on Black Mountain Road and the parking area is at the end.

Parking also exists at the end of Jericho Road, which begins on Route 302, 1 mile west of its junction with Route 16, and at the end of Town Hall (Slippery Brook) Road, which begins 1.5 miles east of the intersection. Many other trailheads also have space to park.

Bike Shops:

The Bike Shop, Mountain Valley Mall Blvd., N. Conway, (603) 356-6089

Joe Jones Ski & Sports, Main St., N. Conway, (603) 356-9411, Rentals Available

Red Jersey Cyclery, Route 302, Glen, (603) 383-4660

Sports Outlet, Main St., N. Conway, (603) 356-3133, Rentals Available

USGS Maps:

Crawford Notch Quadrangle, N. Conway Quadrangle

Additional Information:

White Mountain National Forest, Saco Ranger District, RFD 1, Box 94, Kancamagus Highway, Conway, NH 03818, Tel. (603) 447-5448

Jackson Ski Touring Foundation, Inc., P.O. Box 216, Jackson, NH 03846-0216, Tel. (603) 383-9355

23
White Mountain National Forest
Cherry Mountain

Mountain biking in the shadow of Mount Washington naturally involves, in addition to spectacular scenery, pedaling up big hills and coasting down long descents. The Cherry Mountain area is no exception. As the Presidential Range towers above, deceptively small foothills present marathon climbs and provide a true test of endurance for bicyclists. Spread over many miles, the biking is geared toward longer rides.

The Forest Service actively promotes mountain biking in the Cherry Mountain area and is monitoring its effects on soil and vegetation. Positioned at the northern edge of the White Mountains, it is an ideal place for riding because the trails get little use. Although much of the described mountain biking is on gravel roads open to car traffic, be prepared for complete solitude.

Bounded by the Ammonoosuc River to the south and the Israel River to the north, the riding straddles a ridge of land dominated by the elevations of **Mount Martha** (3554'), **Mount Deception** (3658'), and **Mount Dartmouth** (3721'). Two mountain roads cross lowpoints on this ridgeline and combine to form a popular, 28-mile loop, with other trails offering side trips and alternative routes.

Beginning at the parking lot on **Route 302**, ride the **Lower Falls Trail** up the gentle grade beside the Ammonoosuc River. Halfway along, the gravel road passes **Lower Falls** where the river spills off ledges into a great swimming hole. One mile from the parking lot, the trail ends at **Cherry Mountain Road** which climbs for 3.5 miles and gains 600 feet in elevation from Route 302. The first mile is a steep grind but the remainder is more gradual with occasional flat sections providing helpful rest. The scenery varies from dense forest to open meadows and several clearcuts allow views to surrounding mountains.

Elevation at the highpoint is 2188 feet, and descending the northern slope is a welcome relief. The road passes a few cabins at 4.5 miles, then emerges on smooth pavement and open farmland at 6 miles, one mile south of **Route 115**. Turn right on this highway and follow its broad shoulder to **Valley Road**, on the right beside a set of railroad tracks. Valley Road loses its pavement after a half-mile and winds alongside the Israel River in open farm fields, giving nice views of the Presidential Range. After 3.5 miles on Valley Road's level ground, turn right on **Jefferson Notch Road**, at the approximate midpoint of the loop.

Jefferson Notch Road returns to the National Forest and the shade of the woods within the first half-mile, passing several dead end logging roads as a gradual, 3-mile climb begins. The road has more serious grades for the final 2 miles before it reaches the highpoint at **Jefferson Notch**, elevation 3009 feet, with a gain of 1652 feet from the bottom. This elevation gives the Notch Road the distinction of being the highest public highway in New Hampshire. Mount Jefferson looms above and the **Caps Ridge Trail** leaves for its summit, but the route is unsuitable for bicycling. The 3.2-mile descent on the south side is less steep but still requires careful braking, with the last mile being a fairly flat journey beside the sculpted sluiceways and pools of Jefferson Brook.

The paved **Base Road** was built to provide access to the **Cog Railway**, which has carried passengers to the top of 6293-foot Mount Washington since 1869. Turn right and it is mostly a downhill coast for 4.5 miles back to Route 302, then turn right to return to the parking lot, 2 miles ahead.

Mount Mitten Road provides a shortcut to this loop, reducing the total distance by 5 miles but adding the rougher surface and steeper grades of a trail, so it requires a higher level of riding ability. To find this route, turn right on **Mill**

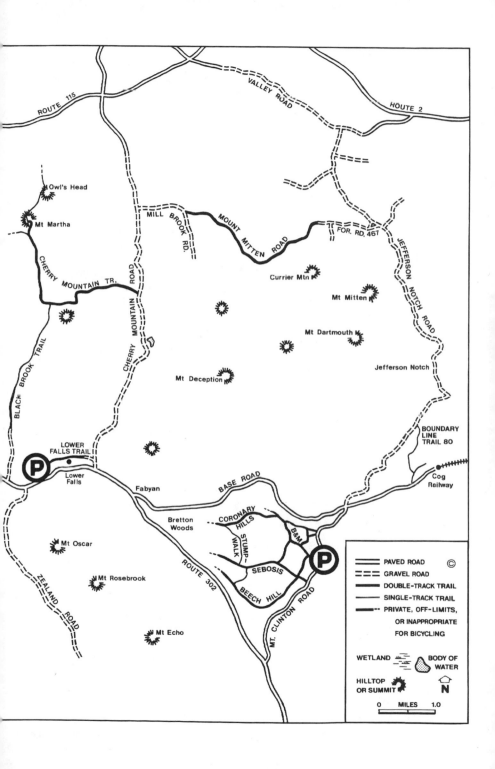

Brook Road (Forest Road 93) 1.5 miles north of Cherry Mountain Road's highpoint. The road dead-ends after 2 miles but halfway along a small wooden sign and a brown, metal gate mark the Mount Mitten Road on the left, beside a clearcut. The next 4.5 miles are grassy double-track with sizeable hills and several areas hindered by ruts and wet spots. A steep descent then gives way to flat ground and smoother pedaling on **Forest Road 467**. Although several marked snowmobile routes intersect along the way, they are rough and overgrown.

If you still have some energy after reaching the highpoint on the Cherry Mountain Road, the **Cherry Mountain Trail** provides a demanding but worthwhile side-trip. It is a relentless, but rideable, 3.7-mile climb to the summit of **Mount Martha** with few obstacles in the way. At 3.5 miles the trail forks and the Cherry Mountain Trail descends to the left. Bear right at this intersection and the cleared summit of Mount Martha is only 0.2-miles away. This last section is a steep scramble but the view of Mount Washington and the Presidential Range to the east and Mount Lafayette and the Franconia Range to the southwest makes a spectacular panorama. Neighboring **Owl's Head** is reached by a narrow path which is best left for hiking.

The engaging **Black Brook Trail** links Cherry Mountain Trail with Route 302, creating an option for a 10.5-mile loop from the parking area. Meant only for skilled mountain bicyclists, this little-used footpath descends through the forest for most of its 3.5 miles and should be ridden in the north-to-south (downhill) direction. Although rocks and bumps pepper the surface, experienced riders are able to find smooth lines through the obstacles. Toward the bottom the trail becomes double-track and slows with more rocks and forest debris, the result of logging operations in the area. It enjoys smooth gravel for the final mile and drops through several clearcuts and logyards to the paved roadway, 1.6 miles west of Cherry Mountain Road.

South of Base Road is an area of National Forest

trails used by the Bretton Woods Ski Touring Center in winter for cross country skiing, but note that not all trails are open to public use since the resort owns much of the neighboring land. From the parking lot on **Mount Clinton Road** look for the trails heading downhill on the opposite side of the road. **Sebosis** and **Coronary Hills** both get regular use in summer and provide good riding as they gently descend to the west. Sebosis meanders for 2 miles over a grassy surface before meeting the National Forest's boundary marker, clearly visible at the side of the trail. Various loops can be made on these trails, but avoid **Stumpwalk** which gets boggy at the midpoint. Other trails like **Porcupine Lane** and **Clinton** are not often travelled in summer and are deep in tall grass, but still rideable. Signs clearly mark the intersections.

Driving Directions:

From Twin Mountain drive east on Route 302 for 2.3 miles and look for the Lower Falls Trailhead on the left, two-tenths of a mile past Zealand Road.

To reach the parking on Mount Clinton Road, continue on Route 302 for another 2 miles and turn left on Base Road. Drive for 4.5 miles and turn right on Mount Clinton Road, and the parking is 1.3 miles ahead on the left.

Parking areas also exist at the tops of the Cherry Mountain and Jefferson Notch Roads.

Bike Shops:

Littleton Bicycle Shoppe, 6 Main St., Littleton, (603) 444-3437

Tobin's Bicycle, 129 Main St., Lancaster, (603) 788-3144

USGS Maps:

Mount Washington Quadrangle, Crawford Notch Quadrangle

Additional Information:

White Mountain National Forest, Ammonoosuc Ranger District, Box 239, Trudeau Road, Bethlehem, NH 03574, Tel. (603) 869-2626

24
White Mountain National Forest
Kilkenny Valley

While most of New Hampshire's outdoor adventures center on the grandness of the lakes and peaks to the south, the Kilkenny Valley sits alone in the far northern reaches of the White Mountains. One of the least-visited, most remote parts of the National Forest, Kilkenny is a wilderness protected by its own set of mountains, drained by sparkling streams, and blanketed by forests which are home to abundant moose and deer. Hunting and fishing account for much of the area's use, but hiking and biking opportunities are plentiful on a variety of trails. It is a natural choice of riders yearning for a truly backcountry experience.

Although some of the roads get regular use, many others are seldom traveled so be prepared for complete isolation and plan to be self-sufficient for your water, food, and repairs. Riding alone is not recommended. Visitors should also be warned that occasional logging operations occur in the area, and that trucks and other heavy equipment sometimes use the roads. Fortunately the cutting has been kept away from most routes so visual impacts are minimal. Mountain biking is discouraged during the late fall when the area's rich habitat is the focus of hunters during deer season, but one of the best times to ride Kilkenny is the early fall when the bugs are no longer biting and the colorful foliage has already appeared.

The Kilkenny Valley's many streams flow into the Upper Ammonoosuc, a river named with the Abenaki Indian word meaning *fish place*, so it is fitting that it be the home of the **Berlin Fish Hatchery**. Located on the shore of **York Pond**, it is New Hampshire's largest hatchery operation and raises over a million trout and salmon annually to stock in streams and ponds throughout the state. **York Pond Road** brings visitors to the facility where a network of pools and raceways make an interesting sight. Fences surround and protect the fish populations, and the staff asks that you not feed or disturb them. Also beware that a gate blocks York Pond Road just before the Hatchery and is open daily between the hours of 8:00 and 4:00. If you drive through be careful to exit before it is locked.

Several hiking trails begin beyond the hatchery at the end of York Pond Road and ascend to various peaks and notches on the ridgeline above. Each starts in mellow terrain and eventually reaches grades too steep for bicycling. The **York Pond Trail** leaves opposite a long, concrete pool of fish and is a technical ride for about a mile before the terrain takes its toll. The little-used **Bunnell Notch Trail** follows an overgrown logging road to several clearcuts while it climbs to a pass beneath Terrace Mountain, 2.5 miles away. **Unknown Pond Trail** is laced with exposed roots and is unfit for bicycling.

Bog Dam Road, also known as Forest Road 15, is ideal for mountain biking as it makes a 15-mile loop off York Pond Road and intersects the Kilkenny's best trails. Well-graded with gradual hills, the road provides an easy means of experiencing this vast wilderness. Mileage markers appear beside the road and are displayed on the map to plot progress. Bog Dam Road begins at the **Kilkenny Guard Station** and runs southward along the banks of the rock-strewn Upper Ammonoosuc River for the first 1.5 miles, then climbs with a series of moderate hills, each separated by a welcome flat or gentle downhill section. The road crests near the 5-mile mark and takes a rolling course for the next 7.5 miles while reversing its southerly course back to the north. Most of the final 2.5 miles are a gentle downhill slope to the western terminus at York Pond Road, only 2 miles from the parking area. Although on weekends an occasional car or two will pass, the road offers all the solitude of a distant trail.

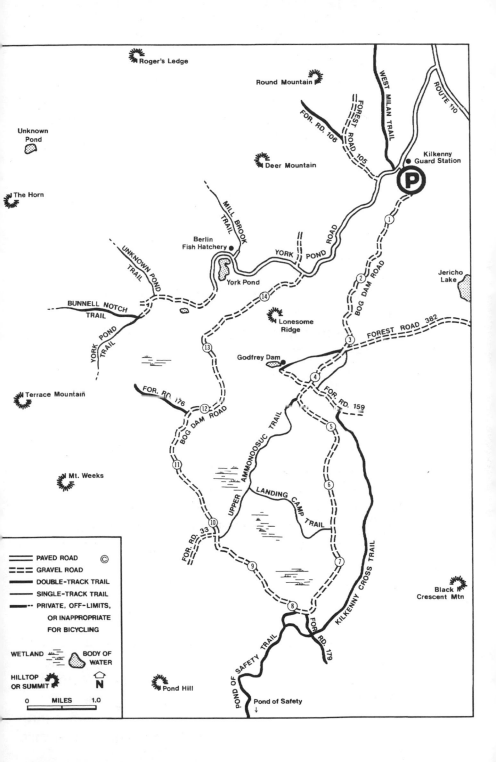

Roger's Ledge

Round Mountain

WEST MILAN TRAIL

ROUTE 110

FOR. RD. 106

FOREST ROAD 105

Unknown Pond

Deer Mountain

Kilkenny Guard Station

P

The Horn

MILL BROOK TRAIL

Berlin Fish Hatchery

YORK POND ROAD

1

BOG DAM ROAD

Jericho Lake

UNKNOWN POND TRAIL

York Pond

2

BUNNELL NOTCH TRAIL

14

Lonesome Ridge

3

FOREST ROAD 382

YORK POND TRAIL

13

Godfrey Dam

4

Terrace Mountain

FOR. RD. 176

12

BOG DAM ROAD

FOR. RD. 159

5

UPPER AMMONOOSUC TRAIL

Mt. Weeks

11

LANDING CAMP TRAIL

6

10

FOR. RD. 33

7

9

KILKENNY CROSS TRAIL

Black Crescent Mtn

8

FOR. RD. 179

PAVED ROAD ©
GRAVEL ROAD
DOUBLE-TRACK TRAIL
SINGLE-TRACK TRAIL
PRIVATE, OFF-LIMITS,
  OR INAPPROPRIATE
  FOR BICYCLING

WETLAND   BODY OF
                    WATER

HILLTOP
OR SUMMIT   N

0   MILES   1.0

POND OF SAFETY TRAIL

Pond Hill

Pond of Safety
↓

Logging has long been a part of the area and many side roads tail off Bog Dam Road into the woods. Some have long been forgotten and are too overgrown for bicycling, but others are gated and numbered and offer interesting diversions from the main road. The longest is **Forest Road 382** which intersects near the 3-mile marker and runs easterly toward the trails of **Jericho Lake**, where the city of Berlin maintains a park and recreation area. The road has a firm surface and moderate hills, and follows the course of an underground water pipeline which was once part of Berlin's water supply system. Dating from 1928, the gravity-fed pipeline begins a mile above its intersection with Bog Dam Road at **Godfrey Dam**, but riding this upper section is difficult. The dam and small pond can be reached by an easier road farther ahead.

Highly recommended is the ride up to the **Pond of Safety**, where a group of deserting American soldiers reportedly hid during the Revolutionary War. A 7-mile roundtrip from Bog Dam Road, the ride requires good leg strength and intermediate skills, although a few spots are difficult. The **Pond of Safety Trail** is well-marked on Bog Dam Road near the 8-mile mark, where it begins a 2-mile hill climb as a double-track woods road, gaining 500 feet of elevation before topping the ridge. It then drops through a more open area for a mile and intersects a spur on the right leading to the pond. Cupped high in the mountains and far removed from the outside world, the Pond of Safety is a pristine sight worth seeing. Continuing straight at the intersection leads to Shag Hollow Road in Jefferson.

The **Kilkenny Cross Trail** is a snowmobile route stretching for 5 miles between Forest Road 382 and the Pond of Safety Trail. It offers a mixture of conditions including treacherous rocky sections, overgrown meadows, and smooth gravel. The local snowmobile club has marked intersections and built bridges to span stream gullies.

The most challenging riding is found on two hiking trails inside the loop of Bog Dam Road. Near the 4-mile marker the **Upper Ammonoosuc Trail** descends as a double-track to meet the Upper Ammonoosuc River, then narrows to a footpath and follows it upstream. The openness of the area allows fine views of **The Horn**, **Roger's Ledge**, and other mountains of the surrounding Pilot Range, a collection of summits named by early travelers on the Connecticut River who depended on them as navigational landmarks. After almost 2 miles the **Landing Camp Trail** joins on the left and offers the best route back to Bog Dam Road, 2 miles away, since the western end of the Upper Ammonoosuc Trail is bogged by extensive wet spots. Both are technical trips requiring skill, patience, and much carrying.

Driving Directions:
   From Route 16 in Berlin, follow Route 110 north for 7 miles and turn left on York Pond Road, marked by a sign for the Berlin Fish Hatchery. After 1.5 miles turn left at the Kilkenny Guard Station on Bog Dam Road (Forest Road 15) and park in the open clearing ahead. Roadside parking is available at trailheads throughout the area.
Bike Shops:
   Croteau & Son Bicycle, 507 Main St., Berlin, (603) 752-4963
   Moriah Sports at 101, 101 Main St., Gorham, (603) 466-5050
USGS Maps:
   Percy Quadrangle, Mount Washington Quadrangle
Additional Information:
   White Mountain National Forest, Androscoggin Ranger District, 80 Glen Road, Gorham, NH   03581, Tel. (603) 466-2713
   Berlin Fish Hatchery, RR#3, Box 3783, Berlin, NH 03570, Tel. (603) 449-3412

25
Nash Stream State Forest
Stark

The north country is a great place for a fat-tire ride. Clean air and mountain vistas are easily appreciated from the seat of a bicycle, and both are plentiful at Nash Stream State Forest. Encircled by mountains in some of New Hampshire's most remote territory, Nash is a paradise of backcountry roads branching through a protected watershed of 40,000 acres. Most remain abandoned since few people venture this far north.

Note that the season for bicycling at Nash Stream is relatively short. The snowmelt lasts a little longer this far north and the ground remains soft and muddy throughout spring. The state forest's roads are consequently closed to vehicle traffic during this period. Likewise, the temperatures in September can seem downright winterlike. Also beware that this is not the place to ride during the late fall, when deer hunting is the primary activity.

Nash Stream Main Road provides the only vehicle access to the state forest and is open to regular traffic throughout its 11-mile length. Though difficult to notice at the side of the road, mile markers are posted to help plot progress on this long ride and originate at the visitor sign 0.5 miles from Emerson Road. The road begins by meandering beside Nash Stream at the base of the valley, paralleling the flow at some points and bending in an independent course through the woods at others. It is an enjoyable trip for bicycling, tempered only by the dust raised by occasional passing cars. The sparkling pools of Nash Stream are fortunately never far away and offer instant relief on a hot summer day. Hill climbs are sparce and brief, and the open space of the road allows good views of the surrounding mountain scenery. Near the 1-mile mark travellers enjoy a glimpse of the unmistakable **North Percy Peak**, whose bald summit resembles a dome of granite. Tree-covered **South Percy Peak** sits closeby and is easily viewed on the return trip. Take a few minutes at the 5-mile mark to enjoy **Pond Brook Falls**, where Pond Brook provides a unique display as it spills over a broad, smooth ledge before cascading into a pool below. It is reached by a short walking trail from a turnout where the road crosses the brook.

The road crosses Nash Stream at the 8-mile mark, passes the **Sugarloaf Trail** which ascends **Sugarloaf Mountain**, and then begins a long hill climb to reach **Nash Bog**. It narrows near the bog where a small community of private cabins overlooks the open expanse of wetland. These camps, as well as others found throughout the Nash Stream tract, are privately maintained and occupied under a unique licensing program with the state. The road climbs steeply beside the rocky course of Pike Brook to a locked gate at the intersection of **Nash Stream Headwaters Road** and **19.5 Road**, which continue for a purely backcountry riding experience.

The only other route open to regular vehicles, **14.5 Road** leaves Nash Stream Main Road at its midpoint and links several renowned trout fishing ponds. The intersection is clearly marked. The road begins with a strenuous, 2.5-mile climb, forks with a gated side road, then continues for another half-mile to the boat launch at **Little Bog Pond**. From this point **Trio Ponds Road** scrambles into the woods with a surface ruptured by rocks and speckled with puddles. A technical ride for bicyclists, it has become badly worn from four wheel drive vehicles and should not be used if conditions are wet. The road tackles big hills on its 1.5-mile course to the first of **Trio Ponds**, where a few cabins sit beside an otherwise pristine shoreline. A 0.3-mile spur leads to the abandoned shores of **Whitcomb Pond** where a collection of fishing boats attests to a healthy trout population.

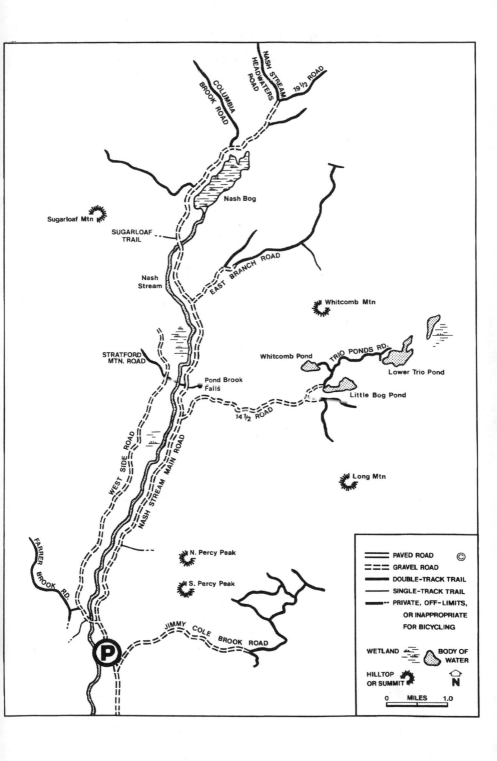

NASH STREAM HEADWATERS ROAD

19½ ROAD

COLUMBIA BROOK ROAD

Nash Bog

Sugarloaf Mtn

SUGARLOAF TRAIL

Nash Stream

EAST BRANCH ROAD

Whitcomb Mtn

STRATFORD MTN. ROAD

Whitcomb Pond

TRIO PONDS RD.

Lower Trio Pond

Pond Brook Falls

Little Bog Pond

14½ ROAD

WEST SIDE ROAD

NASH STREAM MAIN ROAD

Long Mtn

FARRER BROOK RD.

N. Percy Peak

S. Percy Peak

JIMMY COLE BROOK ROAD

P

PAVED ROAD   ©

GRAVEL ROAD

DOUBLE-TRACK TRAIL

SINGLE-TRACK TRAIL

PRIVATE, OFF-LIMITS,
OR INAPPROPRIATE
FOR BICYCLING

WETLAND   BODY OF
                        WATER

HILLTOP
OR SUMMIT   N

0   MILES   1.0

Less than a half-mile from the visitor sign, **West Side Road** crosses a bridge over Nash Stream for the first leg of a 10-mile loop. Bicyclists will find plenty of solitude on this little-travelled side of the stream, along with a constant series of ups and downs requiring a high level of energy. The gravel surface is fortunately broad and well-drained. Near the top of the first hill **Farrer Brook Road** forks left and continues northward for a smooth half-mile before degrading to an overgrown snowmobile trail, and offers nice views of the Percy Peaks from several meadows. West Side Road rolls for another 5 miles before intersecting **Stratford Mountain Road**, a grassy and somewhat overgrown double-track. Although West Side Road continues for another mile before ending, turn right at this junction, identifiable by a wooden sign reading, *Stratford Bog via J. Antritz Trail.* The trail becomes narrow and overgrown but soon descends to Nash Stream, which can be easily forded at low water. Do not attempt this route in spring or during periods of high water. Once across, follow the road to reach Nash Stream Main Road opposite the Pond Brook Falls trail, and turn right to return to the starting point, 5 miles away.

East Branch Road begins 6.5 miles from the sign at an orange, metal gate. It penetrates some of the state forest's most remote territory, winding up a long, gradual hill beside the East Branch of Nash Stream. After a mile of smooth gravel the road enters an open area and degrades, becoming impassable to vehicles. Moose traffic makes some sections choppy with hoofprints, and deep washouts and tall weeds make the remaining 2.5 miles both a difficult climb and a tricky downhill return. A few cleared areas show Sugarloaf Mountain and other surrounding elevations, with beautiful foliage in the early fall.

Another quiet corner of the state forest can be enjoyed from **Jimmy Cole Brook Road**. Although this ride reaches brilliant mountain views, it involves a grueling uphill struggle and should only be attempted by the fittest of bicyclists. It begins with 2 miles of steady uphill pedaling, then rolls for another mile before forking left as a double-track trail. Grass-covered and buried in woods, the trail then climbs for another mile to a second intersection where a 2.6-mile loop can be made. Be sure to explore the spurs diverging from this loop to enjoy the best views, which include the Percy Peaks rising to the north and the White Mountains cutting the horizon to the south.

Driving Directions:
From Route 3 in Groveton, follow Route 110 east for 2 miles and turn left on Emerson Road (4.3 miles west of the village of Stark). Drive for 2.1 miles and turn left on unpaved Nash Stream Road, then continue for a half-mile to the state forest boundary. Park on the grass by the large wooden sign and trail map, or beside the road at trailheads.

Bike Shops:
Croteau & Son Bicycle, 507 Main St., Berlin, (603) 752-4963
Moriah Sports at 101, 101 Main St., Gorham, (603) 466-5050
Tobin's Bicycle, 129 Main St., Lancaster, (603) 788-3144

USGS Maps:
Percy Quadrangle, Dixville Quadrangle

Additional Information:
N.H. Division of Forests and Lands, North Region Office, Lancaster, NH 03584, Tel. (603) 788-4157

Appendix

BICYCLE ORGANIZATIONS

Eastern Fat Tire Association (EFTA), 245 Old Coach Road, Charlestown, RI 02813. EFTA is a non-profit organization of off-road cyclists dedicated to ensuring regional trail access, promoting events for both recreational and competitive cyclists, and promoting responsible riding through education.

International Mountain Biking Association (IMBA), Route 2, Box 303, Bishop, CA 93514, Tel. (619) 387-2757. IMBA's efforts center on assisting in the creation of local clubs and organizations, advising in trail policy controversies, and providing education for riders as to proper standards of safety and responsibility. Annual dues are $15 and members receive the newsletter *Land Access*.

National Off-Road Bicycle Organization (NORBA), 1750 East Boulder Street, Colorado Springs, CO 80909, Tel. (719) 578-4717. The governing body of mountain bike racing and observed trials, NORBA offers a $25 annual membership which includes a racing license and insurance at sanctioned races, as well as the monthly *NORBA News*.

New England Mountain Bike Association (NEMBA), P.O. Box 380557, Cambridge, MA 02238, Tel. (800) 576-3622. NEMBA is a non-profit organization dedicated to promoting land access for mountain biking, maintaining trails open to mountain biking, and educating riders who use those trails to ride sensitively and responsibly. Members receive *NEMBA News* with the latest information on trail access and a calendar of New England's upcoming races, recreational rides, and trail clean-up dates. Annual dues are $10.

BICYCLING MAGAZINES

Bicycle Guide, 744 Robel Road, Suite 190, Allentown, PA 18103, Tel. (215) 266-6893

Bicycling Magazine, Rodale Press, Inc., 33 East Minor Street, Emmaus, PA 18049, Tel. (215) 967-5171

Bike Magazine, Box 1028, San Juan Capistrano, CA 92629, Tel. (714) 496-5922

Dirt Rag, 181 Saxonburg Road, Pittsburgh, PA 15238, Tel. (412) 767-9910

Mountain Bike, Box 7347, Red Oak, IA 51591-0347, Tel. (515) 242-0291

Mountain Bike Action, Hi-Torque Publications, Inc., P.O. Box 958, Valencia, CA 91355, Tel. (818) 365-6831

Mountain Biking, P.O. Box 16149, N. Hollywood, CA 91615, Tel. (818) 760-8983

WEATHER INFORMATION

National Weather Service, Municipal Airport, Concord, NH, Tel. (603) 225-3161

OTHER ORGANIZATIONS

Appalachian Mountain Club, P.O. Box 298, Pinkham Notch, NH 03581, Tel. (603) 466-2725

National Forest Campgrounds, Tel. (800) 283-2267

New Hampshire Campground Owners Association, P.O. Box 320, Twin Mountain, NH 03595, Tel. (800) UCAMP NH or (603) 846-5511

New Hampshire Department of Resources and Economic Development, Division of Parks and Recreation, P.O. Box 856, Concord, NH 03301-0856, Tel. (603) 271-3254

New Hampshire Department of Resources and Economic Development, Division of Forests and Lands, P.O. Box 856, Concord, NH 03301-0856, Tel. (603) 271-3457

New Hampshire Fish and Game Department, Drawer TP, 2 Hazen Drive, Concord, NH 03301

Society for the Preservation of New Hampshire Forests, 54 Portsmouth Street, Concord, NH 03301, Tel. (603) 224-9945

White Mountain National Forest, P.O. Box 638, Laconia, NH 03247, Tel. (603) 528-8721

IMBA Rules of the Trail

1. Ride on open trails only.
2. Leave no trace.
3. Control your bicycle.
4. Always yield trail.
5. Never spook animals.
6. Plan ahead.

Take only pictures and memories
and leave only waffle prints

- -

To order *Mountain Biking New Hampshire* or *Mountain Biking Near Boston* enclose $12.95 per copy, plus 5% sales tax for Massachusetts orders, to:

Active Publications
P.O. Box 716
Carlisle, MA 01741-0716

NAME: _____

ADDRESS: _____

_____

NUMBER OF COPIES: ____ *MOUNTAIN BIKING NEW HAMPSHIRE*

____ *MOUNTAIN BIKING NEAR BOSTON*